THE
MARKETING
GROWTH
FORMULA

The Marketing Growth Formula
The Playbook for Building a Profitable & Thriving Business

Heidi Hattendorf

Published by Game Changer Publishing

Paperback ISBN: 978-1-968250-24-9
Hardcover ISBN: 978-1-968250-25-6
Digital ISBN: 978-1-968250-26-3

GAME CHANGER
PUBLISHING
www.GameChangerPublishing.com

Gratefully dedicated to my family, friends, and
God—for inspiration and support, always.

Thank you to the publishing team for your guidance and collaboration, and
to my many friends, family, and colleagues whose insights, encouragement,
and belief in this work helped me bring it to life.

Praise for *The Marketing Growth Formula*

"Predictable, profitable growth requires the right systems, strategy, and execution to properly scale. *The Marketing Growth Formula* delivers a clear playbook that helps business owners create leverage, so they can spend more time working on the business, not just in it."
—**Zander Woodford-Smith**, Founder & CEO, The Business Coach Academy

"*The Marketing Growth Formula* shows how aligning strategy, technology, and relationships drives outcomes. Heidi provides a timely and strategic guide for GTM leaders."
—**LingRaj Patil**, VP of Marketing, Armor Code

"In an era defined by AI, cloud analytics, and precision targeting, the way we execute marketing has transformed—but the fundamentals of branding, positioning, and segmentation remain as critical as ever. This book brilliantly bridges classic marketing principles with today's data-driven world, making it essential reading for modern marketers."
—**Amy Genender-Feltheimer**, Director of Azure Data & AI, Microsoft

"*The Marketing Growth Formula* is the kind of clarity most businesses don't realize they need until they're already stuck. Heidi distills decades of experience into a refreshingly practical guide that connects strategy to execution, people to process, and vision to value. As someone who specializes in brand, I especially appreciate how this book helps companies move beyond surface-level messaging to build marketing systems—and market positions—that actually serve the business."
—**Ema Davis**, Brand Strategist & Creative Director

"Technology and AI can elevate your marketing, but only with the right strategy, quality input, and strong data at the core. *The Marketing Growth Formula* nails this, showing how technology helps deliver results with the right direction."
—**Norine Martini**, President & CEO, NWI Business Solutions

Read This First

As a thank-you for purchasing and reading my book, I'd love to share some additional tools and resources you can start using today to help plan your business. You'll also find details to schedule a welcome call.

Scan the QR Code Here:

themarketinggrowthformula.com

THE
MARKETING
GROWTH
FORMULA

The Playbook for Building A
Profitable & Thriving Business

HEIDI HATTENDORF

FOREWORD

As a business leader today, you probably feel the pressure to grow faster, work smarter, and align your teams in a world that continues to change at lightning speed.

I've experienced this firsthand as a marketing executive, then as the founder of Terminus, and now as co-founder of GTM Partners, where we help companies of all sizes reimagine their approach to Go-to-Market. The companies that succeed don't stand still or react. They rethink how they grow.

Through this work, I've built two $100M+ businesses and have seen what separates the companies that grow predictably from the ones that stall out. It comes down to clarity, alignment, and the ability to execute, not in silos but as one operating system. That's why this book and the voice behind it matter.

Heidi Hattendorf brings a rare blend of strategic vision and operational depth. She understands how marketing drives business impact and how to activate its full potential within the broader GTM operating system. She helps leaders connect the dots between customer insight, product value, and market momentum. Her work sits at the intersection of strategy and execution, with measurable results.

We are living in one of the most dynamic periods in history, and certainly in business history. Artificial intelligence, automation, and modern tech platforms are completely transforming how work gets done and how we interact and relate to one another. Remote and hybrid teams are now the norm. The barrier to entry for launching new products and businesses has been significantly reduced. The old playbooks are being thrown out.

Growth isn't guaranteed. Markets shift fast. Teams need more than inspiration; they need direction, a repeatable approach, and a formula.

Businesses of all sizes are investing in the latest tools, upgrading their tech stacks, and scaling faster. Yet even with all this innovation, many companies still find themselves stuck. Sales cycles drag on. Messaging doesn't land. Teams feel disconnected. Growth plateaus.

The reason? It's not a technology problem, a sales problem, a marketing problem, or a customer success problem. It's a shared Go-to-Market problem. I've written about this in my best-selling book, *MOVE*, and invested in the GTM Operating System that is now used by thousands of companies. Marketing delivers more strategic value than ever, shaping growth in today's AI-powered, digital, and connected world through clarity, purpose-driven stories, measurable impact, and momentum across the business. This book provides leaders with the tools to make that shift real.

At GTM Partners, we've championed a new way of operating, one that's cross-functional, measurable, and scalable. In any function, teams can confuse activity with impact. They launch campaigns without clear positioning. They automate without alignment. Sometimes they treat marketing like a set of tactics instead of a growth-driving function. The reality is that tools can accelerate your business, but only if your strategy, people, and processes are aligned behind a common goal.

I've had the opportunity to work with hundreds of companies as the co-founder of GTM Partners. I've seen what happens when marketing is an afterthought, and what's possible when it becomes a driving force for brand and revenue. GTM is the business strategy.

And Marketing drives revenue growth by connecting the right product to the right customer at the right time through effective channels.

That's the shift Heidi makes clear in this book. She brings years of hands-on experience leading marketing and GTM initiatives across enterprise companies and startups. But what really sets her apart is how she bridges strategy and execution. She doesn't just share theory, she shows you how to make it work inside your business.

We are at one of the most significant inflection points in history, in some ways the "stone age of AI" – the very beginning relative to what's possible. And yet, growth and success still come down to something more timeless: knowing your market, aligning your teams, and a true connection to your customer. This book helps you balance modern tools with human insight and relationships. That's where the magic happens.

Whether you're a C-suite executive seeking alignment across functions, a business founder focused on growth, or a savvy marketing professional aiming to drive more strategic impact, this book offers a clear roadmap. Heidi brings frameworks, stories, and sharp insight to guide you.

Marketing was never about "doing" more. It's about doing what matters. With the right strategy, clear positioning, and a unified go-to-market approach, growth becomes not just possible but profitable.

Let's MOVE!

Sangram Vajre
CEO, GTM Partners
Author, MOVE: The 4-Question Go-To-Market Framework, a WSJ and USA Today best-seller

TABLE OF CONTENTS

INTRODUCTION

Marketing and growing a business today are almost unrecognizable compared to even a few years ago.

There are entirely **new expectations, new tech, new models, new channels, and new markets.**

The game has changed.

But the core principles? They haven't changed; the focus has. In the rush to adopt what's new, it can be easy to drift from what *actually drives growth*: understanding your market, solving real problems, adding value, and creating meaningful relationships with the people whose lives and businesses your solutions are designed to improve.

And too often, there's no clear path connecting strategy to measurable results. Leaders look to "build their brand," "capture leads, "or "get more content out." Yet not all have a strategic plan to drive a profitable way forward and create actual growth with a purpose.

This book is here to help by offering a formula that blends the underlying timeless principles with forward-thinking innovation.

As a CMO and Go-to-Market (GTM) leader, I have seen this transformation firsthand. I've been fortunate to work with amazing companies and brands, and have seen so many changes in the way we approach the market. I've spent the last 25 years leading marketing, business development, and go-to-market strategy and teams across industries, from global enterprises to fast-moving startups.

The experiences are so valuable across industries too, whether in technology, telecom, life sciences, SaaS, professional services, or manufacturing. In each market, there are common threads to understand the market opportunity and size, and formulate a strategy. I lived and worked for over a decade in Europe, leading global teams and businesses. Today, I help companies through my own company to align marketing and Go-To-Market to drive business growth. My work blends strategy, technology, AI, process/systems, and a human-centered approach.

Given the changes and rapid shifts in technology, connecting people, and innovation, it is an exciting time to grow a business, start a business, or improve a business.

We are only in the beginning of what is to come with AI (artificial intelligence), quantum computing and blockchain. And yet, with all of these technological shifts there is an even greater cry for human connection, deeper understanding, relationships and context.

From a business standpoint, we need a way to blend these timeless fundamentals with what's next. We can use today's models and technology to amplify purpose, build trust, and connect more deeply.

I'm here to collaborate with others to build something amazing together. I want to help you build your business profitably by using the best marketing approach for *your* business.

The most effective strategies are shaped by real-world experience. I wrote this book to bridge the gap to what Marketing can be: a focused, results-driven force that uses both timeless principles and tech-forward tools to drive clarity, business impact, and truly reach customers. This book shows how to build a strategic engine, rooted in timeless principles and powered by modern tools, to reach the right customers and grow.

We'll get to the core of what matters, combined with a blend of more innovative and transformational ways to grow your business. **Marketing is part of the larger Go-to-Market (GTM) engine and a key growth driver.** And you will actually save energy by focusing on the right areas.

The Marketing Growth Formula is designed to help you align to the foundations, put the right systems and frameworks in place, and set up for consistent success. By having the right clarity and focus, you will be able to drive measurable results and profitability with a thriving business.

Whether you're an entrepreneur, executive, or leader, you've likely seen the "perception" of marketing fall into one of two camps:

1. Deep focus on creativity, brand, and storytelling, which is important but only part of the equation. Those outside of marketing might even have a dreamy view of creating advertising taglines or beautiful websites as marketing. This first extreme is a company heavily invested in branding and the creative side, but may lack the systems to convert that interest into business and show measurable results.

2. Deep focus purely on metrics, measures, and the "scoreboard." This is where the pendulum swings to the other extreme, all measures, but limited stories, brand, and context. The plethora of CRM tools and funnel movement has given us more data than ever. But it can be a one-dimensional scoreboard without building context.

The truth is that we need *both* a powerful brand telling a story and performance analytics to measure the impact. Success lies in thinking less about marketing's function and actions and focusing more on the business driver that marketing brings to create a revenue footprint, tell a story, and communicate complex ideas in simple terms. You don't just keep up when you strike this combination; **you lead.**

Taking it a step further, we need a compelling story that resonates with our market, and a system to deliver it through the right channels with measurable impact. *The Marketing Growth Formula* gives you the structure to do exactly that.

Yes, Marketing drives new business, revenue, and growth as part of the GTM machine. The formula is a mix of complete clarity of your company's purpose, problems you solve, who needs those problems solved, and how to best reach them.

The playbook for building a profitable and thriving business links marketing to the business's core and brings us back to our purpose. Simon Sinek famously said, "Start with why." Our brands tell great stories and evoke human emotions. We build relationships with our customers. It's healthy to have a profitable business and to continue investing in its growth.

Regardless of the massive shifts in technology, function, and industry over the last few years, and even over the last few decades, the "how" may have changed but not the "why." Companies are still seeking solutions to their problems, and people still need to buy.

Early-stage growth needs marketing to shape the story from the start. And don't wait until preparation for an exit or sale to "dial up" marketing. The most successful companies are already leveraging the formula to drive profitable growth. Scaling your story requires a clear, intentional strategy.

While I draw on proven tools, from messaging frameworks to go-to-market models, I tailor and apply them to customer needs. Over the years, I've developed my own approach that blends strategic insight with practical execution tailored to each client's growth stage and goals. This book reflects that integrated, flexible mindset.

Throughout the book, we'll have a structured plan for your approach to get repeatable results by combining human ingenuity with winning processes and the best technology, all wrapped together with a measurable plan. Here is a snapshot of the formula, which we will cover throughout the book and in detail in Chapter 7:

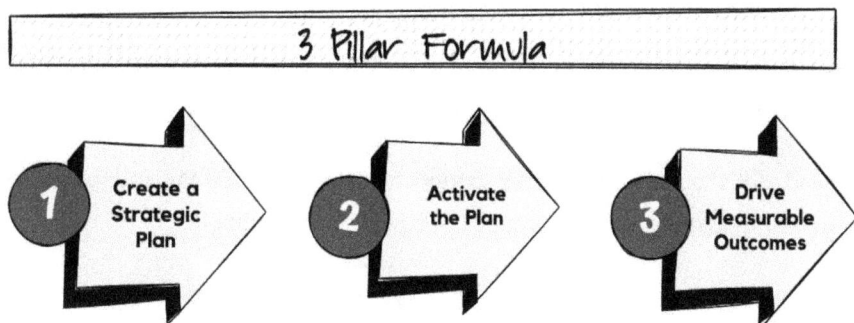

3 Pillar Formula

1. Create a Strategic Plan
2. Activate the Plan
3. Drive Measurable Outcomes

Let's Grow Together

I'm passionate about purpose and growth: growth at all levels, whether it's in business, learning, relationships, or faith. To grow, you need to have a vision and a plan. Then it takes consistency and commitment to execute and deliver on that plan.

Whether you're a business owner, an executive, a marketing leader, or someone who wants to learn and help their business, you'll find frameworks and insights here to help you build smarter and execute better through intention.

Marketing and GTM can help companies move fast. Customers are changing how they buy as digital and social channels continually evolve. Many business leaders I work with partner to expand their marketing and GTM reach to accelerate results.

Sometimes we hear a perception that marketing = social media posting or marketing = a tradeshow or advertisement. That's only a small part of the equation, and certainly not the formula.

That's where a strategic approach comes in. You need a plan before you can implement it. Otherwise, you risk reacting to trends or jumping on tactics without a clear outcome. Too often, companies buy a service, but it doesn't align with their market, audience, or business goals. That's wasted time, budget, and opportunity.

Instead, let's build a plan that connects marketing, GTM, and business growth; not just theory, but practical, proven, and profitable.

Why a Marketing Strategy Matters

Marketing strategy connects your business value to how your market experiences it. With it, you're leading. And too often, marketing can become reactive, driven by shiny objects, chasing a trend. Or, on the opposite extreme, it can be too heavy. Replace the 50–100-page marketing plan with a one-page executive summary that aligns your message, audience, goals, and channels. Yes, there will be the details behind it, and an appendix with pages, but keep it to something everyone can rally around. One-pagers win here.

It's time to rethink how we approach marketing, not as a department or a series of campaigns, but as a **strategic lever** that supports your broader mission. We need a clear roadmap. I want to help you with that, all backed by proven principles, practical tools, and a deep understanding of how marketing, sales, and business success are connected.

You can profitably build businesses by using the best marketing techniques, focusing on **timeless core skills, and the best tech and models.**

From there, you build. Execution becomes easier. Teams align. Partners understand your priorities. Budgets are invested wisely. And results become quantified and repeatable.

This book shares my process for developing that kind of strategy and executing it effectively across marketing and sales. We'll cover how to identify the right levers to pull, how to create a steady drumbeat of connection to your market, and how to measure what matters most.

I'll highlight the timeless principles that matter even more in an AI-driven world, starting with the human side of marketing. Automation should support relationships, not replace them; partner with technology.

GTM involves the full lifecycle from market evaluation and positioning to channel selection, execution, and customer engagement, aligning teams to deliver value and drive growth.

GTM Partners, a data-driven go-to-market analyst firm, takes a holistic approach to the concept of rallying all revenue-facing teams: "GTM is a transformational process for accelerating your path to market, with high-performing revenue teams delivering a connected customer experience."[1] Marketing plays a critical role in bridging strategy and execution. This book will walk through how to build and execute marketing strategies that connect seamlessly to your broader GTM process.

Who This Book Is For

This book is for business leaders who want to build or grow a business. Marketing and GTM strategy can be your edge; the sharp, intentional path to standing out and scaling up. It's for anyone who wants to get to the *heart and soul* of their market and connect with purpose.

---

[1] Karthi Ratnam, "Go-to-Market (GTM): A New Definition," *The Marketing Journal*, October 10, 2023, https://www.marketingjournal.org/go-to-market-gtm-a-new-definition-by-karthi-ratnam/.

There's a reason the word *market* is at the core of both *marketing* and *go-to-market*. Our goal isn't to promote our stuff but to truly engage, to meet our market where they are for a longer-term relationship. Whether you're running a growing company, leading transformation within a larger organization, or guiding others as an advisor or consultant, there is something here for you.

You'll find frameworks here that connect **strategy** to **execution**. If you're a marketing leader ready to level up and lead with greater confidence and clarity, this book gives you a strategic foundation. Advisors and consultants who want a proven structure to guide clients through smarter go-to-market plans will also benefit. And if you're an intrapreneur building something new inside an established company, this book offers a practical roadmap to gain traction and buy-in.

It will help you shift to a more strategic perspective, clarify your message and market, align marketing and sales around shared goals, and build a plan. If you're ready to start building real momentum, you're exactly who this book was written for.

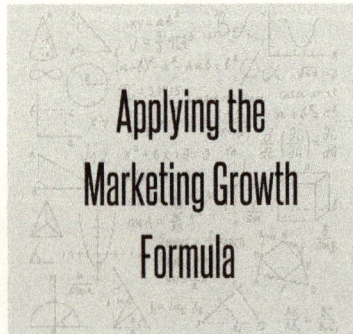

Applying the Marketing Growth Formula

Together, let's apply the Marketing Growth Formula :

- Move from reactive to strategic
- Clarify your market size and opportunity
- Align around shared goals

- Build a plan that's actionable and effective
- Understand your customer to uncover real pain points
- Position your offering with clarity and purpose
- Evaluate the options for a go-to-market strategy that drives results
- Select and use the best marketing channels for your business
- Leverage AI and automation to work with your human team
- Create a repeatable formula for long-term success
- Enjoy your business!

Driving Innovation

My career has mostly centered on business to business (B2B). I've worked across multiple industries and continents, including eleven years based in Madrid and London, leading global teams and working across cultures and time zones. That international perspective shaped how I see the world and how I lead. Understanding cultural nuances, different buyer behaviors, and how technology influences connection is in my DNA.

There are so many similarities across industries when it comes to core strategy. I've advised entrepreneurs through startup incubators, served as a board member for innovation hubs, and mentored university students on customer discovery, business modeling, and marketing planning. I've also coached business leaders one-on-one, helping them scale, pivot, or reposition for sustainable growth. In the end, each organization truly wants to be relevant, provide value, and build something great.

I have a deep appreciation for technology and automation, including the promise of AI. We are in the very early days of AI in the spectrum of what's possible, despite the rapid advancements. I firmly believe tech must serve the strategy and purpose, not the other way around.

My passion for global business has taken me to over 100 countries, and living abroad gave me not only perspective, but an appreciation for connecting across cultures.

What Will You Gain from This Book?

The book is not about adding to the hype or finding a quick solution. The reality is that the "formula" is remarkably straightforward. You'll learn how to uncover your customers' real pain points and design a marketing plan that solves them.

This book helps you move from high-level vision and ideas to practical execution and outcomes. You'll be able to create a plan, measure progress, and adapt as needed, without starting over every time.

One of my core strengths is turning strategy into action, not just handing over a vision but helping you make it work. This book reflects that. You'll get a real-world approach to marketing that meets your business where it is and helps it grow. I don't claim to have all the answers. Instead, I can share my insights, experiences, and approaches based on continual renewal.

My wish is that you'll appreciate the true power of Marketing and GTM to reach your goals, find your customers' pain points, and that I can help you provide a solution to solve those challenges.

If you can help your customers, then serve *their* customers, it's the ultimate pay it forward. Together, we can convert strategy into action. Typically, you're going to see a lot of experts out there who have a great strategy, *or* they can help you with a single tactical part of the plan, such as companies that specialize in a specific area. It's not enough to create a strategy; I also help you turn it into a very actionable, practical plan that gets results.

Inspired and Applied Learning

I want you to be inspired and equipped. My hope is that this book sparks ideas and, more importantly, helps you apply them to your business. You may want to free up more time in your day for innovation, business planning, or spending time with your family. Profit comes in different forms.

I see our work here as a starting point, a foundation upon which we can build your business plan together. Then, let's have a discussion. Let's take it further.

In this book, I will take you on a journey through these key elements: understanding your market, positioning your brand, product, or service, developing a go-to-market plan, and finding the best channels to reach and communicate with your ideal customers. The foundational element of people and relationships, especially in a busy, automated world, is getting results, looking at the right metrics, and then understanding performance to inform strategy and next steps.

Then there's technology: How does it fit in? What about AI and automation? What marketing tools do you need? And what's next for your business? We'll tie it all together.

The first chapter will help you get started because your business deserves a strong foundation, strategy, and growth.

Marketing, when done right, is a growth engine. It's how you connect with the right people, tell your story, and create value. That's what I want for you.

This is your starting point. Together, we'll shape the formula, which will be created with strategy, fueled by purpose, and built for real-world impact.

Author's note: The scenarios and examples shared throughout this book are based on real-world experiences. Some are composites, aggregated from multiple engagements to illustrate key concepts while protecting confidentiality. Any resemblance to actual companies or individuals is purely coincidental and unintentional, unless explicitly stated.

CHAPTER 1

UNDERSTAND YOUR MARKET

Mapping Your Plan

It's important to have a plan when starting anything new. Having a plan is *mission-critical* when growing your business. Yet, so many businesses don't take the time to create a clear marketing plan.

Imagine going on a hike. Certainly, you would have a trail map. You wouldn't just set out into the woods without one. You would want to know where you were headed. You might see something interesting along the way, but you'll start with that map. It's not that different from a car journey. Start with Google Maps or Waze, and literally "map your way." Again, you may see something interesting. You might have to make adjustments and avoid traffic, but you have a plan going in. It's the same with a marketing plan.

Map your plan

The most successful companies have a strategy and know directionally where they are headed. Then, they make adjustments and changes along the way.

In fact, some of the issues come up when adjustments and changes aren't made along the way. Now, more than ever, with AI and globally connected teams, the marketing and GTM strategy and executable plan set the business on the right path. Surprisingly, you don't have to create a lengthy strategy and plan. In fact, clarity and focus will beat out complexity and delay every time. And, you'll have more buy-in and ability to deliver and reach your market.

Traps Along the Way

There are several common traps that can derail the process of building a clear marketing strategy. One obvious trap is indecision or aiming to get the perfect plan together. Create an Agile methodology or iterative approach to avoid this delay. You will be able to test your ideas directly with customers and prospects for feedback, providing much better information to inform your strategy. For example, the approach your team takes with current markets and the customer base will be much different than expanding into adjacent areas, which could require a completely new channel, such as events or digital outreach.

Another common trap is moving in too many directions; it creates the illusion of progress while scattering your efforts. Chasing a long list of initiatives spreads your marketing thin and weakens results. What often happens is that companies chase what they think is marketing, or the "next big thing." It's all well-intended, but suddenly the list of events has grown; there are new outreach efforts, even entirely new audiences to reach.

The popular phrase "Squirrel!" refers to the tendency to dash after something that moves quickly, like a shiny object. It's a clear metaphor for running after something because it's "hot" at the moment. In marketing, this could be a team suddenly switching to quick videos because they "heard" it's the new trend and they don't want to be left out (also known as FOMO, fear of missing out), but it does not tie to their market and how their buyer consumes content. It's a one-off.

To overcome this pitfall, **create a more holistic plan that's strategically thought through.**

This makes sense, right? People gravitate toward shiny objects and run after the "squirrel" to avoid getting left behind or having a competitor move ahead. There's a fear of missing out and how fast the world moves. It's healthy to take on board the latest trends, see what's working, and adjust course. You don't want to be caught in the past, but you also don't want to chase everything. I like the saying: "You can do anything, but you can't do everything."

When looking at the latest on social media, sometimes I see companies overspending on ads or having an ad hoc approach. I call this approach "random acts of marketing." They're really missing out on the chance to **tie together those channels** for a consistent, cohesive message.

Random acts of marketing ➠ not a strategy

Customers may see you showing up in different ways. A consistent message helps reinforce the message, while random acts of marketing do not.

Basically, before trying to do more, I always recommend starting small and moving on from there once you get results. Test your hypothesis to see what's working. Where are you getting a return on your investment, and where do you need to switch course or maybe let go of something?

Another pitfall is a lack of measures, metrics, and data to even know what's working. The good news is that there are more tools than ever to assess what's working and measure your results.

There's a significant difference between chasing after a trend that may or may not apply to your business and having a clear strategy and plan. Regardless of what industry we serve, we are also consumers. We are exposed to interactions in the consumer world, whether it's on Facebook, television ads, or e-commerce one-click ordering. We have expectations from these experiences that trickle over into B2B. We can take those learnings and apply them to the market we are in. For example, if you are selling in B2B, your channel is probably more likely to be LinkedIn or an industry event. Yet, there is social pressure to show up in other channels, which may not even apply to the ideal market.

How do you get started with a marketing plan? It's really important to build a baseline. Look at your current situation. Where are you today? And where do you want to go? Very simply put, what is your plan to get from point A to point B? That's important because you want to measure where you are today, things like your market share, your revenue, your profit, and what type of customers you are addressing. Is that even the type of customer you want to be serving?

Maybe you're starting a business, expanding, or scaling. You could be adding a product or a service line. Maybe you're fixing some issues or turning a business around, and you're trying to get back a market. Define where you are today and what your baseline is, and you're figuring out where you want to go. What are your goals, quantitatively and qualitatively? Once you've done that, it's time to gather market intelligence.

Market Intelligence

This is not about you, your product, or your business. Instead, we are looking at the macro environment around you. What are your potential customers experiencing and seeing in their world? What are their problems? What you offer is within your control, but there are other factors outside of your control.

Let's start by exploring the **external environment** before diving into your offering. This helps us understand the world through your buyer's eyes and the context of your portfolio or offering. There are many potential areas to consider. Let's explore a few of the most common.

Economic

The first and one of the most important is economic or financial. The economic environment is critical because it underlines the viability of your market and buyer. As economic factors change, they directly impact your business. For example, consider a consumer looking at where your market is. Is this a luxury item or a necessity? And that's even defined differently depending on how your customer views it.

What are the trends in your category of spending? It's critical for you to understand and get the data. Consider factors like inflation, interest rates, tariffs, and even currency fluctuations. And if you're sourcing labor or services overseas, you need to include your supply chain costs and the cost of goods. From a cost perspective, as well as from a customer perspective, as the currency fluctuates, what's the buying power? Too often, companies can miss the changes and realities of the buying power for their market.

Here's another important question to consider: **Is your market expanding or consolidating?** Have there been a lot of mergers and acquisitions? If so, it doesn't mean you shouldn't address that market, but it's important to understand the impact, and maybe there's even an opportunity. Are there investment dollars coming into your market? That's another key indicator. The point is to assess whether your buyer can afford your solution; that's very important.

In B2B, some solutions are viewed as essential, such as critical software, while others are considered "nice-to-haves." But then, what a software supplier may view as a necessity, a CFO, COO, or even a CMO may consider *nice-to-have*. As a business leader, part of your role is to demonstrate how your solution solves your customers' problems and can be an integral part of their business.

Compliance

Another area is **compliance** or policy. Are there any regulatory changes that could impact you or your business? A great example that's impacting a lot of us is data privacy regulations. The information that can be shared about your customers is changing all the time and varies by country, and you need to be aware of this. Sometimes, people think policy and regulation only impact those serving the government, but the truth is that they impact all of us to some extent. You will need to do some research on the implications of such changes and how they impact your marketing plans or industry.

For example, let's consider physical goods and packaging. What changes are in place that would impact the physical packaging, such as sustainability or materials allowed? The first level is adhering to the guidelines and regulations. The second level is positioning from a marketing or brand standpoint: How can this actually be a positive for your market? Or, when new labeling laws for food and pharmaceuticals were introduced in both the U.S. and Europe, many companies used the opportunity to highlight the transparency and health benefits of their products. This is an example of aligning both compliance and branding.

Data privacy impacts nearly every business globally. The GDPR (General Data Protection Regulation) rules in Europe influenced similar regulations worldwide. An industry-specific example is HIPAA (Health Insurance Portability and Accountability Act), which outlines the rules for sharing personal medical data.

Industry associations are an excellent resource to understand compliance requirements unique to your business. The same applies whether you are selling physical goods or online digital products. You will need to be aware not only of changes in regulations but also of how you can benefit from them by providing even better products or services. A few examples include safety, ethical guidelines, and geography served. You can take what might seem to be only a rule or guideline and exceed it to help your brand stand out in a positive way.

Buyer Behavior: Needs

Next, we're going to explore buyer behavior as part of market intelligence and research, understanding, and discovery. An excellent example here is the mobile versus desktop experience for a buyer. One of the first places companies share their story is through a beautiful website. The company likely envisions a customer at their desk who is able to see all the information in one place and have it all on one page. This does not take into account the number of viewers on phones and tablets who are on the move or don't want to be tied to a desk.

The reality is that nearly two-thirds of buyers (65%) are using mobile devices versus desktops.[2] Even with B2B buyers, a massive number of buyers are looking on their phones. They're in transit, don't want to be tethered to a computer, or they're waiting somewhere and taking the opportunity to view

---

[2] StatCounter, "Desktop vs Mobile Market Share Worldwide," *StatCounter Global Stats*, accessed March 2025, https://gs.statcounter.com/platform-market-share/desktop-mobile/worldwide.

your information. They may be using brief moments between meetings or while waiting in line to quickly search for information or answers. This is a fantastic opportunity for your brand to literally fit into their day, into their head. With the tools available on mobile devices, apps, and AI, more research is possible than ever, from price tracking to competitive comparisons to monitoring reviews or searches.

You can take advantage of that on mobile devices rather than feeling restricted to the computer. It's important to plan for user experience on the smaller screen for usability, but also consider SMS, or text, which is also very popular in terms of communication. Consider adding customer-oriented chatbots to your website to provide instant information and be more available to your market. What is the next opportunity to get closer to your market?

Buyer Behavior: Changes

Being aware of some of those changes, whether B2B or consumer, is really important. The goal is to stay up to date and notice changes in the buyer, or how your market or consumers find information. Just because your buyer acted one way or had certain characteristics five years ago or even one year ago does not mean that it will be the same today or moving forward. In fact, expect that your buyer's needs will be different as technology evolves and innovation brings about further opportunities.

Consider how your buyer is changing, too. Could your prospect be moving on to other roles, or could the roles be moving geographically? For example, products that used to be purchased by the marketing team might now be purchased by a buying team. Maybe the decision has even moved to the CFO or CIO. We're seeing a lot of technical purchases move to the CIO plus business team, which lets them interface with the different departments. That's something really important to review. Another shift is that your ideal customer could be moving from the U.S. to Asia, or from Europe to North

America, for various reasons. You will need to ensure your messaging captures these nuances and your channels are able to cast this wider net.

Truly understand how your buyer is changing, and don't just assume that they will remain the same. They have their own roadmaps, and their needs, behaviors, and roles can and will change.

Industry Considerations

Not only is it important to look at whether the industry is expanding or shrinking, but what are some of the nuances within your specific industry that you need to consider and understand? An example of this is remote work versus centralized or on-site work, and decentralized teams versus hybrid versus on-site. These types of shifts affect buying, which affects labor.

Just being aware of those shifts, both for consumer and B2B, is a critical start. The key is to dig deeper to see the world through the lens of your client or customer, not just through your own. What are they up against? What problems and challenges are they facing? What trade-offs do they need to consider? It's usually *not* always about price and cost. It could be about time, location, regulations, or a number of other factors that we've covered. What pain is the industry feeling? This is an important indicator of how you and your company can tie into their world and help solve their problems.

Competitive

You also have to consider your buyer's choices and alternatives. Put simply, who else offers what you do, and where does your prospect have a choice or a substitute?

I use the word "substitute" because many professionals only consider alternatives as companies that perform the exact same role they do. However, one of the most important points to understand is non-traditional competitors entering the space. Uber did this by disrupting the taxi industry, coming in from a completely different angle and with a different business model and approach.

Substitute solutions answer the question: What else could be done instead of this type of solution? A lot of times in SaaS and software, the "substitute" or competition is the company continuing to do things the same way, or "no change," such as continuing to work off a spreadsheet. A lot of companies that have fancy and sophisticated software products are shocked to see that a customer has been getting by with a spreadsheet or something very manual, a homegrown system. And that's okay. That's part of the hurdle to overcome in convincing the buyer or demonstrating why this is better and really worth the pain of change.

As you're considering pain points, you need to also understand there's pain in making the change because the buyer needs to do things differently, do some training, or make an investment, and that's interrupting their day-to-day operations. If you can influence them to understand the longer-term value, the cost savings, time savings, and benefits that they're going to receive with your solution, that will help. And, of course, take away the pain by making the conversion or switching much easier for your new buyer. I raise this point because it's often a blind spot in these substitution solutions.

Next comes one of the most exciting areas and important aspects of the marketing strategy and business plan: **What challenge(s) do you solve?**

Market Intelligence Summary Table

Market attribute	Scale of impact
Economic	Macro intelligence
Compliance	Macro intelligence
Geographic	Macro and micro intelligence
Buyer Behavior	Micro intelligence
Industry shifts	Micro intelligence
Competitive	Micro intelligence

Table: Market intelligence summarizing areas to consider in planning. Macro intelligence impacts all companies and is less specific to a given company. Micro intelligence is more specific to a given company or industry. Both are important for a scan of the market as shifts take place.

What Problem Do You Solve?

A critical question to ask in this process is, "What problem do we solve?" Frame the problem to scope, dig deeper, and find out what challenges your prospects are up against today. How is this working for the users? What does the financial model look like? Here's a critical one: "Is this a cost center?" Is this something that they have to invest in, or is this a revenue generator for them? That might sound obvious, but again, that's in the eye of the buyer. Buyers, companies spending money on your product or service, are the ones who get to decide this. However, knowing the difference between a cost/investment versus a revenue generator will help you in terms of how you position your solution.

We'll cover more on the positioning, but at this point, it's about understanding the problem from the customer's perspective. I really like this quote by startup veteran and MIT faculty member, Elaine Chen.

"The customer is the expert of their problem, and you are an expert in finding a solution to their problem."[3] *– Elaine Chen, seasoned entrepreneur and educator*

It helps us to stay centered. We are naturally enthusiastic to share what we've built for the market. But that excitement can sometimes overshadow how we position the product or solution for the customer. In the end, we want to understand the customer problem in depth so that we grasp the nuances of their world and any obstacles so that we can provide the right solution. Also important: Are you providing a **painkiller** or a **vitamin**? A painkiller is needed to get out of pain and to solve an issue, but a vitamin is *nice-to-have*.

pain point!

In an ideal market, we would all be buying vitamins and wouldn't need as many painkillers. But that's not what the data is showing from a commercial standpoint, as more painkillers are sold than vitamins. Especially in tight markets, your companies and buyers are more likely to buy painkillers.

---

[3] MIT Entrepreneurship, "How Entrepreneurs Can Conduct Primary Market Research," *MIT Entrepreneurship Center*, accessed March 2025, https://entrepreneurship.mit.edu/news/entrepreneurs-can-conduct-primary-market-research/.

This is a good place to start in terms of thought process. It doesn't mean you can't have a vitamin or a *nice-to-have* item. Sometimes what looks like a *nice-to-have* is actually a must-have for your ideal customer who really needs the solution. Even a premium solution can feel essential when it solves a problem that matters. Price and tier do not define whether a product or service is business-critical; the customer defines the value to the business.

Customer research sparks new ideas

Next, we will get into **customer research**. What does your customer actually say? Start by validating your initial hypothesis, assumptions about the problems and needs, to ground decisions in real customer needs. Even with experience in the market, conversations with prospective customers often reveal nuances that challenge original assumptions. The goal is to understand their situation and environment. How does the prospect describe the problem, and what matters most to them? What are some of the current challenges that they are up against? Then prioritize: what's their number one problem or pain point?

Next, move into more quantitative questions. How much does this cost them in time, money, lost business, and maybe stress? Encourage them to reflect on how much stress or disruption their current situation is creating, whether it's high staff turnover, difficulty retaining employees, or other costly challenges.

The next step will be to quantify the size of the problem: essentially, the opportunity for you and your business. But there's nothing wrong with starting with the qualitative, truly understanding a little bit more about the problem. Too often, marketers forget about the opportunity costs that customers have. While customers may be utilizing their existing resources and understand that time is equivalent to money, are there other areas where they could allocate their time and funds more effectively? Take time to gather feedback about the problem that you want to solve, whether the solution is a service or a product. That's the first place to start, especially if there's already real customer interest in the product or solution.

Assessing if There's a Willingness to Pay

Next, you'll need to take a realistic look at the market value. Look objectively at whether there is a willingness from the ideal customer to pay for the solution. How much is this problem worth solving? We've identified that there's a problem. The ideal customer is articulating their pain and their issues around it, but are they willing to pay to solve it? That's when the business case becomes real. Too often, founders or business leaders get a step ahead, eager about the new solutions without recognizing the lack of willingness to pay at the desired level, or the absence of a substantial market that truly needs the solution.

From here, assess how the solution stands apart from the competition and addresses unmet needs. Certainly, your buyer, your market, will be comparing your solution to the competition. You absolutely do not want to compete on price alone. That usually signals weak differentiation and positions the offering as a commodity. Even low-cost leaders create a wrap-around experience, and they rely on volume to make it work. It's not a strategy to lead with unless the goal is to scale at all costs or buy market share. But even then, it demands significant investment and a distinct point of differentiation elsewhere. Plus, your competitor can simply change their price.

Most business leaders focus on creating clear differentiation in the market and delivering meaningful value to customers. One way to think about this is by building "a strategic moat around your business," a metaphor Warren Buffett used to describe sustainable competitive advantage.[4] In this context, he is referring to the competitive advantages that protect a company from rivals over time.

For example, a local and family-owned business can create a moat around offering a personal, high-quality touch that fosters trust and accessibility. A larger tech company can also use innovation to build a moat around intellectual property, patents, and proprietary technology. The company could deliver a unique experience that customers can't find elsewhere.

"In many cases, customers aren't just buying what exists today; they're buying into the future you represent, and the confidence that your offering keeps them ahead through technology, service, or insight."

That's more than differentiation, it's your *sustainable* difference. And every strong business needs one. So the real question is: "What's your moat?" What keeps customers with you and not competitors or alternatives?

Also, think holistically about the key stakeholders from different perspectives of the business. Stakeholders could be users of your product or service. Investors, influencers, and other business leaders will have different interests. Avoid solely focusing on the users or only on the business case for finance. Instead, consider how the product or service satisfies a number of different stakeholders.

---

[4] Franklin Tsung, "Storming the Castle: What Warren Buffet Taught Us About Moats," *WealthManagement.com*, January 5, 2022, https://www.wealthmanagement.com/financial-technology/storming-the-castle-what-warren-buffet-taught-us-about-moats.

Consider an ERP or accounting program with a great ROI. CFOs and CIOs may support the investment, but the interface has a poor user experience, is clunky, and difficult to use. That can end up costing the company more in other ways: additional training, extra resources, or even layering on other systems to compensate. When users reject the tool and resort to workarounds, the business loses valuable time and incurs additional costs, even if the original proposal meets the budget.

In contrast, an ERP or accounting system may win over users with a great experience. They find it intuitive and easy to use, but it's expensive to implement and maintain, with a high total cost of ownership (TCO) over time. That kind of solution can be just as difficult to sell. In summary, gaining insights from multiple vantage points will help you avoid these scenarios.

Buyers pay attention to multiple factors during the evaluation process. They will pick up on nuances through reviews, referrals, conversations, and overall reputation. Consider not only the immediate needs but also the holistic needs of the organization for "lifetime value" and total cost of ownership.

Lifetime value is the overall value of that account, what's coming to you as revenue. Do you have repeat business or add-on services? What is that worth?

Highlighting the total cost of ownership is a powerful way to demonstrate long-term savings in both time and money for the customer. I always encourage clients to look at those as two key measures. There are certainly many more, but these are valuable to help review beyond a given project or deal.

How Big Is Your Market?

One of the most critical factors in market expansion, launching a new product or service, is to calculate the market size. I encourage clients to look realistically at how big their market is today and the growth rate (or decline rate) for the future. Run the numbers on market size and let the data tell the story. Too often, leaders spend time on the branding and the positioning but fail to take a realistic look at the revenue and return on investment, leaving it to the end. We all need to understand the market and be responsible for the business. The first place to start is TAM, or total available market. Then we move to the served available market, or SAM.

The total available market is everyone who could be in the market for your particular product. The problem with that is that you're not going to be able to sell to that entire group. What's missing is the ability to capture that market and the number of features and capabilities needed.

Too often, we hear of companies presenting to investors with ambitious TAM figures and large opportunity claims. The problem is, the company may not be in a position to serve even a portion of that market due to limitations in size, product capabilities, or market access. They may be able to serve a portion of the market today, but they need to break down the numbers to show what's realistically within reach now, and what future growth could look like through continued innovation. Highlighting massive TAM figures can set unrealistic expectations that the business can't deliver on. High-growth expectations, without a clear execution path, have fueled some of the turbulence in the tech industry.

Strong marketing leaders need to look at factors such as geographic, but also apply what products or services they offer to give a realistic view of what can be captured. I always look at the compounded annual growth rate (CAGR) as a critical measure. If you want to review whether your market is growing, shrinking, or converging, CAGR is an excellent way to view the category over the next several years.

CAGR essentially provides an annual growth rate that makes it easier to compare performance across sectors. For example, the actual growth may fluctuate year to year, rising 3%–5% in some periods, jumping to 10% in others, or even declining. But the five-year average helps create a more stable basis for comparison. This gives investors a realistic picture of the business's financial trajectory and its potential within the broader market.

> *Summarize your macro environment factors*
> **Tip** *to a single "power" page.*

Now let's synthesize the key insights from regulatory and economic factors, to research, customer feedback, industry trends, and broader market drivers, into a **focused one-page strategic view.** This high-impact summary replaces the need for lengthy 20-, 60-, or even 80-page decks and provides a clear, shareable perspective for aligning teams and stakeholders.

Think of this as your strategic executive summary of key takeaways: clear, concise, and focused on what matters most. Keep the detailed analysis as backup, well-organized and accessible, even with hyperlinks if needed. But too much information without clarity dilutes your message, weakens alignment, and can confuse your audience. Overloading with detail is a common impulse. But if you can't articulate it on one page, then you will likely lose your audience by taking so many words to explain it. Create your one-pager, or power page of the market opportunity.

Scenario

Let me give you an example regarding the macro environment. I worked with several clients in the tech and communications sector. We looked at potential use cases where automation could help in front-office applications to help drive revenue through up-sell and cross-sell. Through customer engagement, we found that the more immediate pain point was more in the back office. Processing invoices, hiring, and reporting were all related to reducing manual workloads.

That was the problem to solve. We had to shift the model to focus on cost savings to free up team members to work on more revenue-related work, such as partnerships, tracking roaming charges for operators, and offering new services. But they couldn't even think past this massive pain point on the cost and time that they were spending on back-office tasks with splintered processes and banks of manual entry processors. We basically pivoted and addressed that problem first, focusing on automating the back-office workflow in accounting. Once that was solved, we looked at helping address the front-office opportunities.

In that particular example, customers in the industry were seeing significant cost savings by adopting the automation solutions, which we were able to quantify. We were able to pivot from the original plan by listening to that deeper need. The front office solution was later implemented as the next priority, and then that became a great success as well.

It was exciting, but we had to understand different departments and needs and be able to adjust course from there.

Connect With Your Market

Once you have created the macro view of the market, it's time to dive into your specific industry and market to better understand the needs. You can start with current secondary research and pair that with your own experience and expertise in the space.

Of course, you should also do your own analysis within the industry, such as participating in industry conferences, and talking to prospects in your market. To supplement, follow some of the notable analyst companies, like McKinsey & Company and Gartner, to read articles and reports that are relevant. Social media groups, such as those on LinkedIn, are another great way, especially for B2B, to get a pulse on the latest changes and innovation within your industry.

I always recommend putting together a brief digital survey where you can personally gain insights and do some of your own research. You can use an online research tool and then reach out to a few targeted prospects. There's nothing wrong with sending a direct message on a social media platform to potential prospects to ask for a couple of minutes for a written survey or for a call. Again, being in an industry or networking group is another great way to get this out there.

It's always smart to ask for a referral for the next person to interview. Let's say that you are having a meeting or a conversation with a prospect, and you gain valuable insights. Take it a step further and ask, "Who else do you recommend I talk to?" It could be somebody on their team or a stakeholder in their company. But always ask the question. Remember, these conversations aren't about selling; they're about listening and learning. Never try to push a product or service on these information calls or interviews. Your main objective is to understand the real challenges, nuances, and dynamics within the industry.

It's important to stay on top of what's happening, not only following news, whether it's in *Forbes* or the *Wall Street Journal*, but also being aware of shifts and changes, which make sense anyway.

A lot of these tips and tricks I'm giving you are things that are practical and actionable, even if you aren't adding a new product line or service or starting your own company. Staying current with your market or prospective market sets you up for success now or in the future.

Stay Ahead of Changing Trends

Of course, you want to innovate, but in a way that will work and can be implemented. Follow new trends, but focus even more on what truly drives results. Remember the "squirrel" from earlier in the chapter? We want to avoid chasing after that next shiny object and being distracted. Keep the spotlight on your target market. Identify who the real buyers are and assess whether the current approach aligns with where and how they make purchasing decisions. We'll cover more of that in positioning, but for now, you want to make sure it fits with where your market buys from, who you're selling to, and the characteristics that define the market. Sometimes companies can separate breakthrough innovation into a new product line and then still incorporate iterative changes into the current lines for the customer base. This provides balance between revolutionary and incremental levels of innovation.

It ultimately comes down to understanding and aligning with your market. B2B buyers sometimes look to consumer trends, such as those in retail, for inspiration. But those signals aren't always relevant outside of the consumer space. Clarifying where your buyer shows up can save significant time and money. There's nothing wrong with being on the leading edge or testing a new channel or tactic. But avoid making major investments before validating the approach. It's important to give any new strategy a fair trial. For instance, with paid advertising, a baseline spend is required before you can expect meaningful returns. I often hear companies say, "We'll just try this for a few weeks," but if the investment is too small, then there's almost no chance of seeing a return.

When testing something new, follow industry benchmarks to give it a fair shot, but hold off on going "all in" until you see evidence that your new approach is working. I see companies selling massive social media contracts and platforms, and they may or may not even be the right fit. They sound good on paper, but that may be the perfect solution for someone else. That's why it's so important to start small. Get some results, iterate, and then build on that success.

It's natural to feel overwhelmed by economic changes, regulatory requirements, competitive pressure, and many other factors. However, before we delve into those areas, we want to look at the world through the lens of our prospect. Let's understand their world, their challenges, frustrations, and priorities. This should be the starting point for any meaningful conversation. Instead of leading with our perspective or solutions, we need to first establish a connection and demonstrate empathy for the buyer's situation to gain credibility and insights.

There's nothing more important than understanding your customers, especially their problems and challenges, on a very specific level, before we can apply our solutions to them. We need to first connect on a human level of understanding.

Keep the lens focused on the market, the customer, the problems they have, and how your solution *answers* their challenges.

CHAPTER 2

DEFINE YOUR MARKET POSITIONING

Positioning is an essential ingredient of a strong marketing strategy. It's also another important way to avoid diving into all of the different marketing channels and tactical plans, such as creating exciting ads, events, collateral, and content, before you are clear on your offering.

In the last chapter, we were understanding the macro environment and considerations on how to best approach it. Now we're applying that environment and what we learned about the world that our prospective customer lives in. We are seeing the world through their eyes. We're thinking about how we take what we've done and apply it. How can we solve their problems and pain points? How do we want to show up in the market and be perceived compared to our competitors? We need to think about "a day in the life" of our customer from multiple aspects of their business.

What does positioning mean in Marketing?

"A positioning strategy is a set of actions and processes that are designed to improve the image and visibility of a brand, company, or product."[5] Very simple and straightforward, and it really captures both the company level

---

[5] Product Marketing Alliance, "Your Guide to Positioning," *Product Marketing Alliance*, accessed March 2025, https://www.productmarketingalliance.com/your-guide-to-positioning/.

and product or service level. When we say positioning, we're not just positioning our company; we could be positioning a product, or we could be positioning a service.

April Dunford, an expert on the topic of positioning and author of *Obviously Awesome*, says, "Positioning defines how your product is a leader at delivering something that a well-defined set of customers cares a lot about."[6] This is important because it shows how positioning is a part of the core marketing strategy, and our intention in the commercial market.

I help clients strengthen their positioning to clearly articulate their brand, differentiate in the market, and connect with the right customers. The collaboration sets up a business for success by giving them a clear view of how a company wants customers to see their brand, product, or service in the market. When done authentically, positioning makes it easier for your customer to see how you fit into the market and solve their pain points.

Define your company's superpower.
Tip *What are you exceptional at?*

When I work with clients on positioning, several high-impact conversations stand out. Together, we return to the fundamentals, asking the right strategic questions that bring clarity and alignment. We explore: What does the business excel at? What truly creates value for the customer? Why do customers choose us, and why do they stay? How do we solve the problem better than our competitors or alternatives? And what genuinely sets us apart in the market? These kinds of questions help clients surface strengths they may not have fully recognized and express their value with more clarity and confidence.

---

[6] April Dunford, "An Introduction to Positioning," *April Dunford Blog*, accessed March 2025, https://www.aprildunford.com/post/an-introduction-to-positioning.

Too often, I come across messaging in the market where a competitor's name could be used in place. That is a clear example of unclear differentiation or intense competition. Write down what sets you apart and spend time thinking this through. What other company could replace your name? That's a sign that you need to review how to ensure that your business is unique and is perceived to stand apart.

The way you solve a problem and your personal relationships can be your company's superpower. The differentiator might be expertise from years of experience, a proprietary or unique approach, or a special value you bring to your customer through your solution. Identifying your position in the market is essential, and having the right mindset and approach helps to uncover it before you move forward. Too often, companies just jump to the messaging.

The messaging will show up in all of your channels' content, and can include taglines, brand tone of voice, or the way you say it, creative elements in advertising, video, social media, and the list goes on. Before we develop the messaging, we need to start with a clear positioning strategy, the foundation that shapes how we communicate our value in the market.

Scenario

I worked with several companies that had strong market leadership in their specific niche, but their messaging wasn't reflecting the full depth of their expertise or value. They had the credibility, but it wasn't coming through in how they showed up to customers.

We stepped back and revisited their positioning and strategic foundation. Instead of getting caught up in the specifics of tactical execution, we simplified everything down to a clear, one-page summary of what made them distinct. What we found was that their positioning had become too broad, too generic to stand out, and for a customer to understand what they could provide.

I helped them identify three core pillars that defined their value, why customers chose them, and what they did better than other alternatives. Next, we established the basis for a more powerful brand narrative. This clarity became the core foundation for their broader strategic marketing approach and for crafting messaging that truly resonated with their market.

Once those pillars were in place, everything else became easier to align. The teams could communicate with consistency across channels, whether on social media, at events, or in conversations with customers and partners. The real breakthrough was helping them see their strengths in a new light that translated into new business. As a result, they gained internal alignment, clarity across teams, and sharper go-to-market execution that connected more directly with their buyers.

Successful companies often know what makes them strong, but without a clear positioning strategy, those strengths don't always translate into the value provided, consistent messaging, or aligned execution.

The Substitute [Name] Test

One of the pitfalls, and companies can get this wrong, is making the pillars or value statements too generic. This comes back to the "name test" I mentioned. If you can substitute another company's name over your three pillars, then you have not created something unique to your company or brand. For example, you might say, "We have [X] years of experience." But who else can say the same, and what does the customer actually care about? Do they really value your [X] years of experience, or do they care more about trust, credentials, positive reviews, and referrals?

A more effective approach is to translate what those ten years of experience actually mean for your next customer, whether measurable results, a strong referral base, improved efficiency, or deep industry insight. Highlighting specific examples of the problems you've solved and the types of customers you've served not only builds credibility but also clearly differentiates your offering.

Reaching the Ideal Customer

Thinking about it through the lens of the customer or the client, what does your *customer* care about? When you consider where to start on positioning, start with *who* you are trying to reach. We talked a little bit about that in the last chapter, but now we're going to make it more specific. We call this the **ideal customer profile**, or **ICP**.

What is the ideal business that you serve? The ICP would be your ideal customer who is going to come forward and say, "YES! I want to buy that from you," or "I want to do business with you." The ICP could include characteristics such as the industry, the size of the company, their pain points, or their needs. There can even be a geographic element to increase or decrease the scope, such as accentuating the local aspect or the opposite, emphasizing a national or global aspect to show scale.

I'll give you a few examples. One could be in FinTech: "I want to reach financial companies with over $50 million in revenue based in North America, that are looking for growth in adjacent spaces, and use an RFQ process."

You may or may not need that last point, but we want to make this specific. Another one could be accounting firms with revenue between $100 million and $500 million and struggling with outdated or manual processes. They need automation, and this is going to be an offer aimed at the COO or head of operations.

Now, let's look at a local example, such as a law firm. In this example, we could use a family business, not a chain, with five to ten employees that needs a better way to advertise or bring in professional clients.

As the saying goes, "if you try to sell to everyone, you are selling to no one." Defining your target customer becomes essential. We'll start by narrowing in on company size and the specific problem you solve, then build from there. The goal is to identify your niche, or the segment of the market where you're best positioned to solve a distinct set of customer challenges.

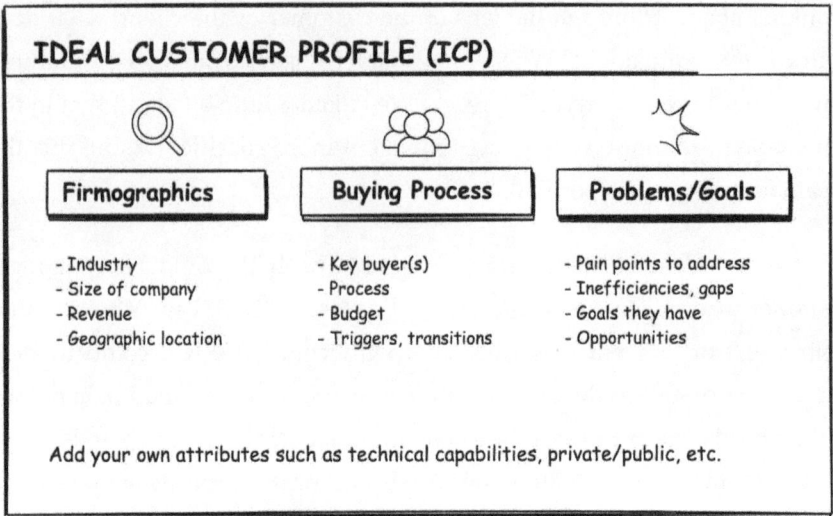

IDEAL CUSTOMER PROFILE (ICP)

Firmographics	Buying Process	Problems/Goals
- Industry	- Key buyer(s)	- Pain points to address
- Size of company	- Process	- Inefficiencies, gaps
- Revenue	- Budget	- Goals they have
- Geographic location	- Triggers, transitions	- Opportunities

Add your own attributes such as technical capabilities, private/public, etc.

This doesn't mean you're limited to selling only to that group, but it's where you can start.

An ideal customer profile is important because venturing into other areas often requires new offerings, different messaging, and alternative ways of connecting with those markets. As a result, your efforts become diluted and less effective.

When you specialize and repeat your offers, you build deeper expertise, deliver stronger service, and create a more scalable business model.

Profitability also matters. Spreading your efforts across different types of offers and markets means you will have to create multiple approaches to reach your markets and spend more on marketing and development of products and services. This also adds more complexity to your product or service delivery and additional strain on your team. In the end, it reduces margins and will exhaust your team.

A focused ICP also means you save the bandwidth of trying to context shift between various markets. Later, you may add other customer profiles. To start, I recommend honing in on the essence of your business, your "bread and butter." Think of your ICP as being on the company level, attributes about the type of organization you want to reach.

Next, we're going to explore the specific person you want your message and offer to reach: the "persona."

Targeting Your Ideal Customer Persona

Your ideal customer is a specific person who would want to see your product or solution and think, Yes, that's what our company needs, or, This resonates; I want to learn more. The target persona represents the buyer you're aiming to engage and ultimately sell to. It's essential to understand who this person is and what matters to them.

For example, in B2B, there's typically a buying team that represents various stakeholders. You will want to consider the user in addition to the actual buyer and have messages that address each of them. You could have the financial stakeholder, the business owner, or even a user as part of the buying team. HubSpot has a really good example: With their targeted CRM platform, they actually gave a name to their target persona that they called "Mary Marketer," which was a fictional representation of a marketing manager or somebody who would be both a user and influencer for their product line.[7] Originally, they were spread over multiple personas, but then they focused in on this key persona, and they were wildly successful with this targeted approach because their positioning and messaging spoke right to the person. This story has been widely documented, and GTM Partners also has a research paper specifically on this case.

Treat the consumer and enterprise/B2B personas differently. In consumer markets, marketers define personas using specific demographic attributes such as age, location, income level, and gender. This level of detail helps align directly with the allocation of advertising budgets. Think about your own experience as a consumer. You might watch certain TV shows, browse specific websites, or spend time on particular social media platforms. Advertisers aim to reach you based on those behaviors and secure media space according to these demographic characteristics.

In B2B markets, it's very different. The personas are typically defined more by roles, responsibilities, business challenges, and decision-making authority than by traditional demographics. For example, we could define the target persona as an engineering manager, CFO, or CMO. In B2B, the goal is to identify the specific individual or role within a company who would be most interested in your solution, whether it's a product or a service. Depending on the offering, that could be someone in accounts payable, a finance lead, an IT manager, or the CIO.

It's less about age or location, and more about understanding what keeps that person up at night, what metrics they're accountable for, and how they evaluate solutions. The focus shifts from broad reach to relevance, speaking directly to the needs and priorities of a specific buyer within a company.

---

[7] ThinkGrowth, "HubSpot's Playbook for Going from Startup to Scale-Up," *ThinkGrowth*, accessed March 2025, https://thinkgrowth.org/hubspot-s-playbook-for-going-from-startup-to-scale-up-29ab85d3a3e1.

The reason that we're identifying the individual or role is that the marketing message needs to be tailored to that person. We want that person to hear it and feel as if it were written for them. For example, we could create this for an IT leader or CIO: "Is your development team overloaded with configuration requests from the business? Our software was designed for business users to free up your IT team with configurable templates. Cut processing time by 20%."

For the buying team, we will have different messages for each aspect, and understand each pain point or challenge. Here is a quick breakdown of potential roles:

- Sponsor: advocate, typically a leader who is trying to solve an issue

- Main user: person or department who will be using the product/ service

- Financial: who is paying (is there department control, or will this need to go through finance, business owner for a small business); tied to the sponsor

- Influencers/stakeholders: or anyone else who is impacted, such as other business teams that have a say or vote in the process; this is very common with a buying team.

Buyer 'Persona' considerations

Job function/title (eg CFO)

Department (eg R&D or Accounting)

Challenges (eg reducing sales cycle)

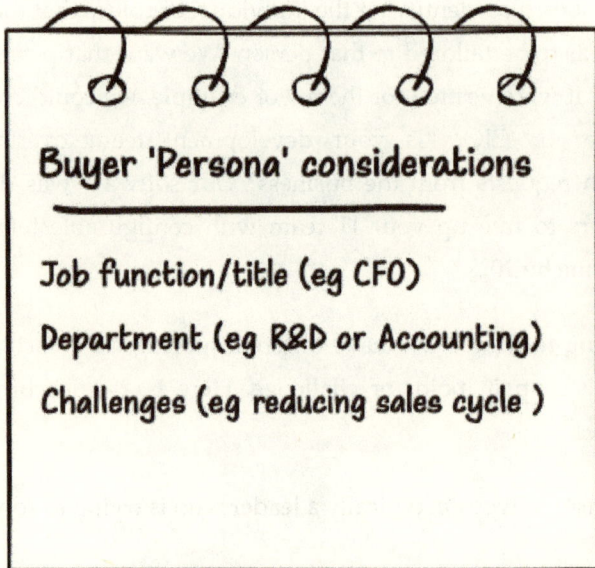

A strong marketing plan begins with identifying the top two to three key personas. Each may require slightly different messaging, but this clarity at the start sets the foundation for more focused and effective execution.

Sometimes, marketers with a consumer background apply the same persona model to B2B, but it doesn't translate as well. For example, they may try to build B2B personas around personal demographics, giving the persona a location, age, or specific educational background. While that approach works in consumer marketing, it's less relevant in a B2B context.

In B2B, focus on the **role** you're targeting, such as decision-makers, influencers, or users, because buying decisions often involve multiple stakeholders.

In business to consumer (B2C), your focus shifts to the **individual or demographic**, tailoring your message to resonate with personal motivations, lifestyle, or behavior.

There is some crossover. Sometimes, you will see enterprise-level apps advertised during a major event such as the Super Bowl or the World Cup. This is an example of a sponsor recognizing that enough of the audience watching are both consumers and business decision-makers. This approach works well, for example, with large-scale enterprise platforms.

Redefine the Space with Your Point of View

Create a "point of view" (POV) to map with your positioning. It's the story you tell about the problem you're solving, why it matters now, and how your solution fits into that bigger picture. A strong point of view can be a strategic stance that clarifies *why* your company exists and *what* it believes about the market. It frames the problem you're solving in a way that often challenges assumptions and invites your audience to see things in a new light. In positioning, your point of view acts as the anchor; it shapes how you define the category you play in, how you differentiate, and how you communicate value. It draws a clear line between the status quo and your vision for what should be.

"Point of view" emerged to help move from selling features and benefits and a transactional approach, to a more cohesive narrative. At the core, you are helping your market see why the current way is not good enough and challenging basic assumptions.

For example, Figma carved out its place by challenging the siloed, static design workflow with real-time collaboration for modern product teams. This is a solution used by many companies for creative development across teams. Think about how Warby Parker entered the eyewear space. The accepted norm was expensive frames sold through optical shops. Their point of view? Buying glasses shouldn't break the bank, and you shouldn't have to leave your house to try them on. I find this ironic, too! Their strongest point of view wasn't just through their eyewear and lenses; it was more about challenging the entire buying experience. That belief reshaped how people thought about eyewear, positioning Warby Parker not just as a product, but as a modern alternative to an ingrained industry model.

Identifying Your Competition

Think back to what we discussed earlier around market intelligence. Who else can offer something similar to your product or solution? What are the substitutes, either a company from another industry or your prospective customer choosing not to move forward with any solution and instead staying the same? Research the market to better understand and look objectively at what competitors provide. The ultimate goal is to meet and exceed the needs of your customers. As part of that process, gain an understanding of your customer and their challenges, plus a view of their options, including other offerings, pricing, and key service or product attributes. This will help your company differentiate and provide unique value.

Start by understanding what your competition offers and the options your customer has to solve their pain points. Business leaders sometimes claim there's "no competition" for a new product or service. That can be true in a brand-new category, but it's rare that there isn't at least a substitute in an established category. More often, they mean there is no direct competition. This is a strong position to be in, but it may also require marketing to educate prospects on a new innovation, category, or approach.

The reason to promote an entirely new category is to get people on board or bring the market along. And that's fine. That's innovation. The reality is that every product, service, or brand was new at one time. But outside of a new category, there is typically someone who can provide at least a substitute for what you're offering, what you're providing. I'm only encouraging you to reflect and explore deeper before moving forward.

From a marketing perspective, and as you communicate it to the customer, it is a powerful technique to show that there's nothing like what you're offering on the market. We need to differentiate our brands and show that our product or service is so different that others really can't compare, which is actually very effective.

However, also take an honest, informed view and be clear about your position in the market. Stay aware of the competition, so you're not caught off guard by how others position and deliver their offerings. This will help you better understand the options from your customers' perspective.

One way to view the other options in the market is to create a matrix of competitors and substitutes. On the Y-axis, you would list key attributes, and then maybe the competitors or the products on the X-axis.

Think beyond features and functionality. What really matters in a buying decision? Include your company brand, whether product, service, or company level. The other extreme is that, too often, companies only list their competitors. Be sure to list your company and at least three competitors. These can be current competitors emerging, or substitute/alternative solutions, such as a homegrown system.

Try to imagine a company coming in from left field, perhaps from a different industry, using a different technology, or offering a new perspective, as a disruptor. What could they do? *If my company were going to disrupt this market, if we were going to come in and invent something, what would we do?* That kind of thinking helps spark creativity, because once you imagine the disruption, you can start to counter it.

COMPETITIVE COMPARISON	Our Brand	Competitor 1	Competitor 2	Substitute/ Alternative
Company size				
Scale (geo)				
Market reputation				
Quality				
Service				
Pricing/ value				
Customer service				
Capability 1				
Capability 2				
New, emerging, established				
Additional points....				

Along the Y-axis, list the different attributes, and along the X-axis, list the competitors. List commentary in each box for comparison. Create a quantitative scale or simply make notations. I like to color-code it. Mark in green where you're strong, red where you're weak, and gray where you're neutral. This gives you an idea of how to map out where you stand and where to take action.

Also, include the approach your company is using today, such as working with a small local agency or using a homegrown software system. If you are offering a service and you see that your potential client is doing the work in-house or planning to cover with their existing team, it could open a new opportunity for you. How could you help them take the pressure off the existing team, freeing them up and creating a better alignment to their core skills and competency? There is a significant opportunity cost they could be missing, especially if the service is not directly in line with their business.

If the prospect is looking closely at your competitors, consider what others in the market bring. Then list the key attributes and objectively look at the other alternatives: How well-known are they? What is their digital footprint? What's their reputation? How are their referrals and level of customer satisfaction? What is their reputation, and what is being said about them out in the market?

Think about other attributes that are important to your buyer. It's about what your customers value, not what each of us thinks is important. Do they care most about quality or do they perceive quality to be about equal in the market? Do they care about speed, ease of use, or expertise? Is this a very specialized area? Only you can name what those key attributes are based on how well you understand your customer. These examples are prompts on some common aspects to consider.

I have used this methodology for a number of years to create strategies based on what the data and comparison information are telling us. Often, companies have this information, but are moving so fast, they may not take the time to write it down or brainstorm with the rest of the leadership team to assess, because they intuitively operate and are busy running the business.

However, it doesn't have to take long, and is actually very strategic. When you collectively evaluate and write down your competitive comparison, you and your team gain new insights:

1. You could be **overcompensating** against the competitor. Once you write this down, you might realize you have many strengths that you're not highlighting or positioning.

2. You could be **underestimating** a competitor. This happens a lot for new entrants. Business leaders may think that they're small and not established, and they get somewhat dismissed.

3. As the executive or business leader, now you can help your team understand these differences and clarify your positioning and messaging to customers. The information will also help inform strategic decisions on where you may need to invest.

Going through this exercise will help you keep your eyes wide open and give you clarity to articulate the difference between what you offer compared to the market. Keep an eye on emerging or new competitors who could come in.

They could be offering great deals to your client base. Maybe they're trying to **buy the market to get in.** But what can you offer that's *different*? You definitely do not want to compete on price. First, it's easy for a competitor to copy. Second, it's a race to the commoditized bottom of the profit curve.

Instead, you could talk about your years of experience and separate yourself through unique backgrounds and expertise that are difficult to copy for a newer entrant. Some companies use **FUD: fear, uncertainty, and doubt**, in their marketing materials when talking about other solutions. But staying focused on your attributes and not mentioning the competition is a way to keep the high ground and not give your competitors free advertising. Stay focused on your own brand's value and how you solve problems to make business and life easier. Educating and guiding prospects to consider attributes such as certain specs, capabilities, or expertise will help them naturally make the right choice.

Your Special Formula Positioned in the Market

Once you have a clear, updated view of where you fit in the market, your position, and your point of view, then you can see where your strengths are and if you are leveraging those strengths in how you're talking about your company. Or do you need to create a specific themed campaign to tell your story? That's all part of your positioning, understanding what makes you valuable and where you can shine. Reviewing the results informs your plan on where you can adjust, but you don't have to react and "fix" everything.

It's really important to be aware and then prioritize what's most critical to take action on and to account for the differences. For example, a software company could be missing key features, but to compensate, they can demonstrate that their product is easy to use and simplifies work. If you truly know the industry, you might say they're missing a lot of key features, or you might decide to add the capabilities in, but it's really up to the buyer. It comes down to what somebody is willing to pay for and truly values.

A good example is a company that provides fast turnaround and focuses on delivery. It might not be the cheapest, but its value proposition is to focus on speed. It's going all-in on that attribute. A similar situation could be true for companies that focus on quality.

Think about how your solution can be unique and show innovation. I really appreciate the book *Blue Ocean Strategies* by W. Chan Kim and Renee Mauborgne.[8] It's a popular book and concept, and it's another way to look at standing out: Make your offer so different that you are competing less because you're separating yourself from the competition.

One of the quotes in the book is: "The only way to beat the competition is to stop trying to beat the competition."[9] The concept here is that instead of competing in this crowded "Red Ocean" or existing market space, businesses can focus on creating new untapped market spaces or "Blue Oceans" where they can innovate, make the competition almost irrelevant, and unlock that new demand. The strategy emphasizes its value innovation, focusing on unique value and then lowering your cost basis for efficiency and to achieve sustainable growth.

Think of the "Red Ocean" as shark-infested waters. It mirrors the blood spilled in this competitive space. It's a graphic analogy because you can imagine yourself swimming away and saying, "Look at how we can solve

---

[8] Blue Ocean Strategy, "What Is Blue Ocean Strategy?" *Blue Ocean Strategy*, accessed March 2025, https://www.blueoceanstrategy.com/what-is-blue-ocean-strategy/.

[9] Goodreads, "The Only Way to Beat the Competition Is to Stop Trying to Beat the Competition," *Goodreads*, accessed March 2025, https://www.goodreads.com/quotes/9712258-the-only-way-to-beat-the-competition-is-to-stop.

your problem in a completely different way." Now, you have the space to articulate your key points and connect with your buyer.

It starts with positioning and thinking about how your product or solution fits into helping and guiding customers who match your ideal customer profile. You're not reacting; you're simply adjusting, and you're looking at the data as a key indicator.

Let's take an example in the consumer space: a high-end sports shoe that has specific materials for performance that really sets it apart from the average tennis shoe or trainer and is clearly aimed at elite athletes. That's a great example of positioning. The company is not trying to showcase a low-cost budget. The brand message is saying this is for elite athletes requiring certain specifications, and the company knows its market. Their messaging and their go-to-market channels will reflect this image, which started with core positioning.

In B2B, let's take an example where the solution is streamlining CRM integrations with sales data and marketing workflows in healthcare. The collaborative software simplifies the process, automates the workflow, and custom builds for different providers with the right regulatory compliance built in for data privacy. This clearly sets the solution apart from a "horizontal solution" that serves multiple industries by solving the more specific problem sets unique to that industry. Part of the software company's positioning in this example is, "We understand your market. We understand how important this is to your customers." The trust factor will be there, and the knowledge of the business.

Sometimes, you hear companies say things such as, "That's all we do. We serve this market exclusively." The underlying message could be: "Don't go with someone who is also working across multiple markets. They don't understand you like we do."

That brings me to another important point. Whether your company is B2B, B2C, or B2G, use certain language, "keywords," and nomenclature that are recognized within the industry. It's not meant to be a code. But in any industry, if you can use specific language and words that demonstrate you have a deeper understanding of the market, then you will have much greater credibility.

Next, we can translate capabilities into what is important for our customers. I like to call it the "so what" test, which is a popular way to test your message. For example, we may hear, "Our service is based on decades of experience." But what does that really mean for the end customer? It could be quality you can count on, or a product that has a unique formula or patent. The customer would have to make the leap between the years of service and quality experience. Why not bridge that gap and cross the finish line for them? Instead, the company could say, "Backed by thirty years of experience working with COOs and business owners, we understand the operational challenges and have built solutions…" In this example, we are applying the experience.

Another example is showing how the product or solution is unique. "You can't buy this from anywhere else." Make a statement and then ask yourself, *So what? What does that mean to my customer? And will that resonate with a buyer, or is that something that has more to do with me?* You've got to really turn it around.

Too often, companies are beating the drum about what they provide, but they're not really talking about what's in it for the customer and in the customer's language. The "so what" test is really a tool or an exercise that can help you flip it around and make it truly about the buyer's needs.

What in your positioning will stand up in the market or not be copied? How would your competitor react? One of the many reasons not to compete on price is that a competitor can change their price tomorrow, and then you're in a price war. This is another reason your market position should also not be based on price. But companies that compete only on features are only one step up from competing on price because your competitor can add a missing feature, capability, or claim. That's why you want to have something more intrinsic, more deeply tied to your purpose and brand. Create that point of view we covered to infuse your brand and position into the bigger story about what's changed and create a compelling need.

You hear companies talk about their brand. Geography can become a natural barrier. For example, your company could be that local company that can provide an unmatched service experience. Branding is a great way to make it intrinsic. Other companies can't simply copy because it is a combination or formula. For example, you can talk about your team providing bench strength and level of service, paired with investments in technology that solve your customers' problems.

You have to be able to communicate that in a way that resonates and clearly articulates why you do business with your company. Many companies use Intellectual Property (IP) as a way to separate themselves, especially in technology. In the last chapter, we covered the concept of creating a moat in business, which refers to something that can separate you from your competition. It's easy to imagine a castle with a moat. This can include patents and trademarks, but it's something unique that others can't copy. Reputation, expertise, quality, and other distinct characteristics help you to differentiate in the market, and you will want to back these up where possible. A few examples you can use: reviews, referrals, references, customer quotes with permission, and being able to demonstrate your company's capabilities, such as a video or demo.

First, think about your positioning, your place in the market, and what makes your company and offer unique. Then, before we get to messaging, think, *Could I back that up with stats, quotes, or a case study?* or *What are my proof points on that claim?* Part of this exercise may be to realize you need to go get some more proof points to build that out. Most businesses are continuously refreshing their stories and case studies to stay current and provide a variety of examples to show breadth and depth in helping their customers achieve outcomes.

Thought Leadership

Now we're going to explore one of my favorite topics in marketing strategy: thought leadership. At first mention, some may dismiss it as vague, abstract or disconnected from revenue. Yet ironically, once they understand its true purpose and impact, it's *exactly* what they want. Why?

It's simple. Humans relate to stories, and the people in the business have a story to tell. They want to make sure that their brand rises above the day-to-day transactions and hustle, and is heard by the C-suite or by business owners. Thought leaders win attention by clearly stating their brand's purpose and story. Sometimes they will include the point of view we discussed earlier, challenging current assumptions and putting forward a better way for the industry.

It truly is the essence of your business. It's that Blue Ocean concept that we talked about: fresh new ideas, a new way to solve problems, and helping your customers through their challenges. It's extremely important. It's an opportunity for a business leader to have a viewpoint, tell a story in a longer narrative, and describe the attributes, such as their vision. Where is the company going? What trends are happening in this industry? How can customers navigate through?

I think the other reason it's become so popular is that it's not direct selling. I love the phrase, "Buyers love to buy, but they don't want to be sold to." Thought leadership gives you a way to educate, inform, and tell that story. You can talk about the industry, the problem set, and solutions without being "salesy." You are contributing to the wider industry. Executives and experts are able to talk more holistically and let people learn about them and their brand, without a "pitch."

Scenario

Here's a great case study. I've helped many customers, clients, and companies with their thought leadership content. Typically, the leadership content will be consumed by executives. That's another reason it's so popular: it's created by the executives or founders for executives and owners.

One person could tell the story, or the team can help shape it together. For example, I worked with a client in the SaaS space on helping their clients with a fintech solution.

Together, we created a thought leadership strategic piece to position and tell the story by defining the problem, looking objectively at how other companies are solving the problem, identifying what's missing in the market today, and informing on what is possible through a compelling vision. The thought leadership paper and point of view spoke directly to executives. It was so well received because it was something they hadn't done in the past and was fresh, alive. We were clear to keep it informational for the market, and not "sell."

We focused less on promoting a solution and more on framing the issues through a broader lens, helping fintech executives connect the dots on *why* these challenges persist and what's driving them across the industry. We worked on a bigger-picture concept around the "why" of the category. If this concept resonates with you, it could be that your market doesn't fully understand why your solution category is important. Alternatively, they may not be aware that there are solutions to these challenges, and "it doesn't have to be this way." The "why" is so critical to understand; you're pointing out some of the pain points and problems that maybe they weren't even thinking of from that perspective, but came at it from a completely different angle.

Other common forms of thought leadership are presentations and podcasts. By design, thought leadership is often packaged up in longer forms to give a leader in a company a platform to position themselves as having these forward-thinking thoughts and establishing authority. The leader communicates, "I can guide you on the way forward. Let me help you navigate this complex space." It's an educational approach without selling, and it goes a long way toward building a reputation and establishing credibility so that target companies in the ideal customer profile see your company name. The target companies then see your expertise in the industry.

Positioning Examples for Brand

When it comes to establishing a brand, positioning is at the core.

For consumer companies, brand investments are massive because the message has to scale to a large group, and the company may not even meet the buyer. Think about yourself as a consumer. You absorb all of these different messages, and the sponsor only has seconds to grab your attention, whether it's an expensive commercial, a billboard, or an ad on YouTube.

It's a quick hit because it's blasting to a massive group. Think of consumer brands that you know well and the feeling that they invoke because they're just trying to get an instant connection and emotion and be *remembered*. A few examples from my experience are:

- **IKEA** empowers customers through accessibility to clean, affordable design. Through self-assembly, you save money without sacrificing style. The consistent look and practical approach have earned a loyal following.

- **Starbucks** isn't about price, it's about experience. It makes everyday coffee feel personal, with handcrafted drinks, seasonal flavors, and turns a daily ritual into a small, rewarding luxury.

- **LEGO** is an innovative brand that fuels the imagination of both kids and adults. With a strong community of fans who share ideas and creations, and constant product innovation, LEGO keeps the experience fresh, creative, and collaborative.

These brands lead by continually evolving and refreshing. They bring fresh ideas to market without losing sight of their core positioning and point of view in the market.

Now, let's look at B2B. Brand is equally important, but it's communicated in different ways. There is a greater focus on the attributes, measurable criteria, and buying teams. They know there's probably a longer buying cycle since these can be larger investments. Here are a couple of examples from my experience and perspective:

- **Slack** is a platform built for collaboration, connection, and efficiency. It brings people together who quickly become part of a shared community with a common purpose. With a large, active user base and no cost to join (for entry-level only), Slack has become a powerful way to foster real-time communication and build communities. That spirit of connection is central to the brand.

- **Salesforce** is a well-known, enterprise-level customer relationship management (CRM) platform focused on organized data, sales pipelines, and business growth. Many businesses rely on the system to manage customer relationships and align sales and marketing teams.

- **AWS or Amazon Web Services**. Cloud power, agility, and innovation. They have built a distinct brand identity separate from

Amazon's consumer and e-commerce business and positioned themselves as a trusted B2B technology partner. Very effective on the B2B branding.

- **DocuSign.** The other example I'll give you is DocuSign. Part of their message is that it's easy, but they also get across the ideas of trust, security, and digital. They certainly solve the pain point of manual effort to print out the form, sign it, scan it, send it, and integrate it with the other pages, or use DocuSign. The word has become synonymous with digital signature: "Send me the DocuSign." It's become interchangeable with the category that it serves.

When a brand becomes synonymous with its category, such as "hand me a Kleenex" instead of a tissue or "let's schedule a Zoom" instead of a video call, the brand has reached a new level. The brand has become the default, both a sign of widespread recognition and a deeper signal of how people engage with the entire category.

Reputation

The last point we'll cover here related to positioning, is reputation. Companies spend a lot of time focused on their reputation for good reason. A stellar reputation can take different forms. It could be reviews, referrals, or specific customer recommendations. It could be vouching in a request for quote (RFQ) for another company. It's definitely the lifeblood of any company. We want to buy from someone others have bought from before and had a good experience with.

Through my business, I've helped several companies with customer surveys. It's really important to get this right and to understand your customers' perceptions of how things are going, what they want in the future, and their top challenges today. It's also an opportunity to uncover new problems that can mean new business and new revenue streams for you.

You're getting a pulse on what your customers are saying and how your market feels. And there's definitely an art and science to conducting these surveys. The companies that I found to be most successful are the ones where this starts at the top with the founder or CEO who has a genuine interest in real, authentic feedback and understands its importance.

There's a difference between an annual or periodic customer survey and quick feedback questions after a sale. For a deeper annual survey, we want to gauge what our customer thinks about the company overall and the relationship. Then, at the product, service, or project level, we want to understand: how did a specific install, implementation, or rollout go? Did the customer perceive value? It's important to have both perspectives. I work with companies that emphasize both because you want to capture that immediate feedback from those involved in the business, but you also want to be able to get an executive-level view and pulse check. Asking your customers to give feedback shows maturity and interest in improving and continuing great service. It also helps flag any issues that could signal problems with retention or renewal and will impact your ongoing business.

Internal culture is very much tied to brand, but what does that entail? How do your employees feel, and how does that permeate out into the market? Top companies are very interested in having a positive and strong corporate culture that translates into a great customer experience.

One of the top questions candidates ask when interviewing for a company is, "What is the culture like?" The reality is that there are going to be different subcultures, especially for a larger company with different departments or locations.

Often, the company itself might have a slightly different view. Of course, they're going to describe it in a very positive way versus what others might say. Both candidates and prospective clients are going to validate what they hear from you with review sites to compare notes.

However, we always need to be aware of how internal culture is tied to the brand. You can't think that you have one brand externally and another for your internal brand. The more a company believes in its mission and lives its values and brand promise, the more likely it is to have a strong culture.

Both the brand and corporate culture start at the top. "The way things are done," the messages and the values communicated to employees and customers will truly permeate throughout. Savvy leaders understand this concept, though other leaders may dismiss it as being "hard to measure."

Some companies have gone the other way and over-indexed on brand and not enough on the hard metrics, such as the conversion of leads into business. When you think of your brand, I recommend you think about both aspects: **reputation**, what people are saying, how the messaging gets through to represent the brand, as well as the hard **metrics**. And then you must also take into account the corporate culture and how people within the company feel about the brand, because that will always spill over into the market, whether positively or negatively.

The brand and market positioning lay that groundwork, and that's going to make it easier to bring in new clients. The best companies understand and invest in positioning, and that's why you hear so much about brands.

Tip *Here's another tip: create a mock press release to align the message.*

If you were to issue a press release about a new product or about your business, what would it look like? This is a simple exercise to help rally the teams and make things very clear and simple by creating a mock press release. The technique was made famous over twenty years ago by Jeff Bezos, but is more widely used now than ever in a busy social media world.[10]

For example, you may be thinking about a new product and its positioning. What will that look like? Imagine what it would be like in seven months. Write the press release now: *"We're so excited to be launching product [X]…"* Of course, you will change it and update it; this is not an actual press release.

Here's a quote from a client who has used this approach: "The press release approach helped us align the teams around our launch and envision success, but also how to describe what we were bringing to the market."

This is a popular exercise that's been used by many companies. It really helps align and motivate everyone, but more importantly, it helps simplify and get your message down on one page. That's really critical, and I think it's an interesting and inspiring way to do it.

Connecting the Dots

To conclude this chapter, I'll leave you with some closing thoughts about positioning and why we do it.

Think back to market intelligence and setting the stage. We looked at what we know about the macro environment, and explored how we fit in. More specifically, we evaluated how our product, service, or company is positioned compared to everything else out there in the market. We're trying to connect *what* we do with *how* the customer sees the world.

We thought about the **ideal customer profile**, who we're serving, and the **persona** within that ideal customer profile, taking into account whether B2C or B2B. Next, we looked at the importance of a **Point of View** in describing

---

[10] Daniel Lotzof, "Why Jeff Bezos' 'Future Press Release' Strategy Matters In 2025," *Forbes*, March 28, 2025, https://www.forbes.com/councils/forbescommunicationscouncil/2025/03/28/why-jeff-bezos-future-press-release-strategy-matters-in-2025/.

the current challenges and putting forth a hypothesis on how things could be better, a challenge to the norm. Then, we looked at how we compete; not only in how we position ourselves but also in how we connect the dots and help our customers see how we're different. We're going to help craft that path and not just leave it to them to decide.

However, we're going to guide them by articulating some of those differences. It doesn't have to be naming the competition. It could just be pointing out some of those differences, separating ourselves with that Blue Ocean, getting away from the Red Ocean, where it's literally a sea of *same*. Next, we're thinking about how we can set ourselves apart, contribute to the industry, and set the direction for where the industry and our solutions to solve challenges are headed.

Finally, we're going to build a **strong brand and reputation**. We're going to use it both internally and externally, and invest in both.

"One of the most important elements of positioning is demonstrating how you solve problems for your customers and can improve their work and lives."

That's the essence of why positioning is so important. It gives you the right **mindset** and **framework** out of the gate to set yourself up powerfully for the messaging and not just dive straight into the messaging and the go-to-market activation. With the right positioning, the message will be heard and can resonate with your market.

CHAPTER 3

MESSAGING THAT RESONATES

Crafting Your Message

Your message is the core idea or value that your market will understand, remember, and act upon. It needs to reflect what matters most about your brand, what you offer, and why it's worth paying attention to. Essentially, it's what you say, and how you say it.

We have a solid foundation of understanding the market and clarity on how our product, service, or company brand is positioned in that wider market. Now we'll look at how to most effectively reach our market with a message that resonates.

What do we mean by messaging? In its simplest form, **it's how you tell your story.** When we talked about positioning, we focused on the framework, mindset, and the "way" we're going to talk about our solution or company. We also included a point of view and framework to challenge the status quo. You might recall that I said that marketers tend to want to dive straight into the messaging before covering the positioning.

Messaging can be creative, shaping the story, refining taglines, and selecting the keywords that resonate. We imagine agencies creating the perfect pitch or tagline, a Madison Avenue-type exercise. In reality, your messaging requires both a creative approach and a technical approach, such as research, to truly align with your customers. When done well, marketing professionals use messaging across formats and channels to build a consistent, cohesive story.

Now, we can start aligning those words to the forums where we'll meet our prospective customers. How are we going to communicate this in a language that will resonate with our ideal customer, persona, stakeholder, consumer, or person(s) we want to connect with to consider our product, service, or company?

The words matter. The images matter. The tone, the vibe, makes a difference. Recall that we talked about industry specifics. Some industries expect you to use specific words, which demonstrates that you understand the nuances of that space.

And to clarify, this is *not* about "cramming your content" with keywords. It's about choosing the right words that naturally reflect how your audience thinks, acts, and seeks. Start with the human connection, and then only later move to the search algorithm. The goal in messaging is humanizing the messaging to use the words, pictures, and messages, or "content," that's going to truly connect with our market. My goal here is to set up the concept of messaging and describe why it is so important to think through the strategy before diving into the specifics.

The right message will also depend on the geographic location and the function or role of the receiver. For example, if your customer is in finance, you will want to use financial terminology in stats and ROI to get through. The size of the company makes a big difference, whether you're talking to a startup, medium-sized company, or enterprise. For example, job titles will vary by size of company as well; a smaller company may use Founder versus CEO or fractional roles as the company grows.

In its most basic form, we want to connect with the market. We want the words to resonate, and we want people to understand what we're saying. That's how your message will connect.

We talked so much before about the problem statement and the problems our customers and buyers have. We want to inspire our prospects to speak with us by demonstrating that we are learning more about them and can solve the problems they are experiencing.

Understand Your Customer

Messaging and content can be created in various formats. The common element is that they are all meant to connect and resonate with the customer, to "click." Ideally, you want them to think, *This company understands my situation* or *They found a solution to my problem.* When all is said and done, you want them to feel understood.

Messaging can also be a powerful way to identify who *isn't* part of your ideal customer profile. For example, if you are targeting a certain-sized company with budget expectations, the messaging may help some companies self-select out. A prospect may see this and think, *That's not for me.* If you have developed a high-quality solution or high-tier product offering or brand, you may come across someone who's looking for a low price, that low tier, and that's fine. They can self-select out to pursue other solutions.

Messaging also serves that purpose. I shared one of my favorite phrases: "People hate to be sold to, but they love to buy." This sentiment is very relevant to messaging. Avoid being overbearing to annoy your audience. In fact, being too aggressive can give sales and marketing a bad name. Think about layering your approach and message. **Don't try to get it all done in one message or one channel.**

In fact, each message builds on and reinforces the other. While positioning sets you up for the right channel, messaging focuses on how to reach your customer or buyer, where to reach them, and what to say.

Reaching Your Market

Now that you understand your market and positioned your company, product, or service, and crafted strong messaging, it's time to bring that message to your market.

In the next chapter, we'll explore how to develop a go-to-market (GTM) strategy that aligns your broader revenue goals and selects the right plays, such as inbound, outbound, events, or a combination tailored to your market. GTM spans the whole revenue cycle, including marketing, sales, customer success, and operations, and comes to life through the specific plays you run to engage and grow your market.

GTM is a strategic approach to reaching your ideal customer. The marketing channel is the tactical execution or way in which we reach them. The message we use will vary significantly depending on where we are reaching them.

Then there is the type of content or materials you will use for the specific channel that aligns to the style most commonly used. The art of marketing is to select the appropriate channel where your ideal customer will be, using words and images that tell a story that will resonate with your market. It's not about making a killer ad or video on social media; it's more important to figure out and create a message that will connect with your audience.

In B2B, you might have an executive interview in a podcast to help a CFO or CEO learn more about the industry and the challenges that need to be solved. Or a company might publish a whitepaper (a detailed, authoritative report a company publishes to explain a product, service, or idea) or blog article on their website for an engineer to download to learn more about a technical service. A consumer goods company might sponsor a radio ad or offer a discount in a print ad or QR code. Social media, much like "media," is too general or broad. It's important to identify the exact channel, align with that platform, and then determine whether your strategy will be to share content, host events, run ads, or use a mix.

To reach our busy market effectively, we need to use multiple channels. Buyers today are so bombarded that they need to see the company brand and message multiple times, in multiple ways, before buying. Many companies invest heavily in that exposure.

Think about both the digital and then the physical world. If you have a store location, then you can have a blend of physical and digital presence. But even for companies that are virtual or online, they can still have face-to-face meetings or events. Think about ways to blend both physical and digital. For example, on your website or in an email outreach, you could offer customers the opportunity to stop by your store or take a tour of your facility. It could be demos of the product, examples, or case studies of services. Don't just think in terms of digital, and don't just think of only the physical world.

Now, more than ever, multiple channels in marketing are essential. This is why so many companies chase after the perceived latest way to reach customers; they continue to be distracted by the "jumping squirrel." In fact, sometimes our biggest threat is not our competition or technical challenge, it's the distractions we chase after. We're going to be selective, and we're going to pick the channels and messages that resonate the most and will give us the best ROI, as opposed to trying to do all of them.

Content That Connects With Your Market

You can continue to build on those deeper levels. Taglines are only part of your whole messaging framework; they are only the tip of the spear. We're going to go deeper, and there will be more meaningful content for greater depth and breadth of our message.

Again, it's like peeling back an onion. We want to frame our message for our audience with the right words, images, and video that will resonate. In digital marketing terms, we want to show up and rank high in a search (be found by our customers), whether it's with AI or traditional search engines. There is an entire industry built around SEO, or search engine optimization.

"Our primary goal is to be found by and understood by our ideal customer, not win an algorithm."

It's important to use specific words tied to your industry or company, called keywords, that will put your organization in a more favorable position to be found online. Your content needs to have industry-relevant words that are intuitive to buyers. The trick is to avoid having your pieces so loaded with keywords that your buyers miss the key points, and it sounds like jargon. Have you ever seen a summary that has the perfect corporate-agreed words but misses "plain-speak" so much that someone reading wonders what it's trying to say? Your market will not take time to unpack the message; instead, they'll move on to a company with a clear point to make.

If you are creating the perfect corporate message, think about "who is that really perfect for?" That's why some of this corporate speak gets a bad name: it doesn't at all connect with the customer. We're seeing this more and more, especially with generative AI and large language models. But even before that, there was a lot of corporate jargon. In other words, there are complaints now about copy being written by AI and sounding robotic.

Yet some corporate messages may also sound robotic! Regardless of how you create your message, it needs to resonate with humans. We are selling to humans. I know I have created some of the "perfect" copy in the past and learned to make it more plain-speak. When I worked overseas, working in a different language and working with customers where English was their second language, it made me more acutely aware of creating plain-speak, more direct language that is understood.

"Ironically, the perfect message is one that your audience understands."

Now, there's a greater need than ever to return to authentic, simple words so that customers understand quickly what's being said and that it resonates.

Let me give you an example in the tech space:

Jargon version:

Our cutting-edge, enterprise-grade proprietary platform leverages synergistic cloud-native architecture to deliver scalable end-to-end digital transformation, harnessing AI-driven analytics and robust security. We empower organizations to unlock mission-critical insights, optimize operational efficiencies, and drive innovation at scale. Our best-of-breed solution seamlessly integrates with existing tech stacks, ensuring frictionless implementation and maximum ROI across the entire value chain.

Hmmmm… that might have all the right keywords for SEO and pass the buzzword test, but it is difficult to grasp. Surprisingly, this example might even sound the same as competitors' text since so many companies will focus on wanting to use the latest buzzwords. These examples are everywhere, and we've all done it at one point or another. Regardless of where it ranks in the search algorithm, it doesn't really matter if it doesn't resonate with our ideal customer. Let's try the same concept, same company, with more plain-speak.

Authentic, human version:

We offer a powerful, unique software tool that's designed for large businesses. It's easy to set up, works well with your current systems, and can grow as your needs change. Our software helps you make better decisions by analyzing your data and streamlining your processes. It's built to be reliable and secure, and our team is here to support you every step of the way. We help your business work smarter and faster through your investment.

Do you see the difference? We're simply using a lot of plain words. We're getting right to the point. The exact approach and wording does depend on your customer and industry. Some buyers may appreciate a little more specific language and actually look for key phrases or specs. In this example, I wanted to show the differences so that you can think about the style and adjust appropriately to your market.

Stories Drive Interest

Another crucial aspect is building and creating content with impact. One way to make your content or message meaningful is through storytelling. If you are telling a story and thinking more about your audience and relationship, then your focus shifts to hearing, learning, listening, and understanding. You can do this through informing, educating, and entertaining, as examples that are less about you selling.

Let's face it: Humans relate to stories. The television and film industry is a $300+ billion market, proving the value of a compelling story. In a similar way, terms like "thought leadership" or "storytelling" can elicit eye-rolls or dismissive looks when marketers use them. How will a story convert into customers? Through human connection and relatedness, interest. By now, this approach is more widely adopted because it directly ties into human nature, winning hearts and minds.

But when you think about great stories, there is usually a pattern. The same is true for brands that resonate; there is almost always some type of human emotion, a tie-in, and it doesn't have to be complicated. There could be a few key characters in your story:

- **There's usually a villain**: This could be the problem or instigator. Maybe it's the outdated software, the overwhelming invoice process, the mountain of payments and manual entries, or the lost time and frustration. That's your villain. I always advise clients to stay away from making the competitor the villain in your story because that's not really who you're up against, right? Think about running in a race. If you're always looking over your shoulder at where your competitor is running, it's going to slow you down. What you want to do is focus on the end game. Be aware of who's around you, but focus on your race; focus on what you can provide in that customer connection, the value you bring. The reality is that your buyer does have many options, not just you or your competitors, and you don't want to do free advertising for your competitors. That's why it's best not to name them. The goal is to overcome the obstacles or "villain."

- **There's a guide**. The guide is the next one. The guide is you, your company, solution, or team. You are acting as a sherpa in the mountains. You're a trusted guide who has walked this path before and knows where the cliffs are, the falling rocks, and the reptiles. Your company is taking the customer on an important journey, arming them with the tools that they need to overcome and defeat the villain. You want them to be the hero. The conflicts are the obstacles standing in the way. It could be *their* competitors, budget constraints, challenges that their customers have, or reputation management. It could even be busy teams that want to avoid a new solution, given the time it will take to cut over. Think about how you have helped other companies with these exact challenges. You're helping them with that conflict and knocking down the obstacles.

- **There's always a hero**. Every good story has a hero. The hero needs to be the customer, the person who is responsible for slaying the dragon or solving the problem or challenge, who faces up to the villain. Too often, I've seen companies try to make their solution, company, or even themselves the hero. "To the rescue... jumping in to save the day." In reality, the hero is the customer who is dealing with the villain or problem. Your hero customer could be armed with your solution or teamed up with your company to guide them. The customer is now equipped with your solution or expertise to help overcome the problem.

If you put it into a storytelling framework, your content is going to be a lot more impactful and relatable, not to mention memorable. This doesn't mean you're naming all of these different roles. Instead, you are connecting at a human level and demonstrating your expertise.

It's subtle, but it's more interesting than a direct sales pitch that might cause your ideal customer to ignore or gloss over it. Think about how popular and memorable TV ads can be; many tell mini-stories, capturing hearts and minds quickly. You might be thinking that a financial person, a technical developer, or an engineer certainly would not tell a story. However, interpreting what the data is telling us, the insights, and the technical possibilities sometimes make the best stories and drive change.

Format for Understanding

The next step is to look at which messaging format will resonate most with your market. At this point, we're really thinking about connecting with our client and what will make the most sense. If you are trying to get across more complex, technical concepts or topics that have references or research and are data-driven, then you may want longer-form content such as a whitepaper or a series of informative articles. Another option for a deep dive to expand on a topic would be a video interview, such as through a **webinar** or **podcast**.

Video also gives the audience a better opportunity to get to know you or your company a little better. It's a way to move from "cold" outreach to "warmed up," to giving your audience insight into who you and your company are and what you are about. For example, imagine the prospective client doesn't really know your company.

Now they can see one of the executives on video or a subject matter expert in a technical video. It really helps compress that "get to know you" phase because the prospect is seeing and hearing the interaction. Podcasts are another really great example. Busy leaders who are traveling or have a few minutes en route or at the gym can "consume" a podcast to get information, get educated, or understand new entrants to the industry.

One of the reasons podcasts have become more common is that, in a busy world of content and with so much written online and on social media, they provide depth through a one-on-one interview. They give the interviewee a stage to share a little bit more and express their ideas and context. This comes back to **thought leadership** → **unpack ideas**. Also, people can listen when they're in the car, walking, or doing something else. That's another reason they've become so popular.

Events are another example. Events are important because you get that face-to-face interaction. Companies used to send team members to industry events. In fact, this used to be one of their main strategies for assessing who is in the space and which companies they would evaluate. Events can be an excellent way to influence through that multi-channel approach. Maybe the prospect is already talking to your company, but seeing your presence at the event can showcase your brand or portfolio. If your client base goes to these industry events, you also need to be there and have a presence. But with the explosion and opportunity of so many face-to-face and virtual events, you can be selective on which will offer the best value for your company, the best ROI.

There are several different aspects to an industry event for content and messaging. One of the core opportunities is for an exhibition stand, which has messaging and can draw attention to your brand and portfolio. Another critical opportunity is for a speaking slot on the agenda to demonstrate industry knowledge or a case study. Perhaps the company sponsors and has a speaker with a presentation providing context for the industry. These are all different formats that content can take to communicate the key messages.

It's important to consider options and think more broadly about format and content. It comes back to how your ideal customer and persona buy and then how they decide. For example, is there a buying team of decision-makers? Is this a more formal purchase, such as an RFQ? Is it a smaller company where relationships are very important, and it's a referral-based decision?

I always recommend to clients that the best strategy is a mix of different formats. That's because your buyers or prospects are going to show up in different places. Prior to meeting with your company, customers are doing their own research more than ever before using reviews, websites, and videos. They may or may not even meet with your company!

Digital Presence

If our prospects are researching our companies online, then we need to have a strong digital presence. For example, check that your website is up to date so customers can find out about your company and do a little bit of research. There is an opportunity to repurpose and remarket your messages and content into different formats and "link" them together. Remarketing examples include embedded links in your content that send users somewhere else for more detailed information, which can all be tracked. Tracking which areas are the most clicked or viewed will give you and your team an idea of where to focus and what resonates.

Don't get caught up in thinking that "clicks" is your final metric or measure. These initial views can be thought of as leading indicators but not the end game. You need to look at conversion rates and how many of the prospects are moving through to conversations and then sales.

When you "repurpose" content, you use one piece of collateral and turn it into other assets in different formats. This provides consistency across channels and also ties together themes. For example, a strong blog or published article could be split out into smaller chunks for social media posting, and then you can point to the larger article for more depth. Pair that with some images, and you've got some really powerful content.

Here's another example: your team writes a whitepaper on using AI for personalization and customer service. It highlights the latest technologies and includes real-world examples. Next, you can easily package the main themes and content into an article or blog on your website to drive traffic back to the full whitepaper and your site. At the same time, you're collecting contact information from your customers where they "opt in." It's a tradeoff: the prospect provides their information, and in exchange, they get the paper. It's critical to follow data privacy rules and give them a chance to see how the data is used and have the opportunity to "opt out."

You could also run a webinar based on the concepts in the whitepaper. I've helped many clients with this as well. There's no reason to have different teams create these parallel efforts. Instead, think of the various formats as sub-elements of the same theme. Also, the themes and tone would likely be different if you used different teams. We are aiming for a consistent, coherent theme across channels to be recognized and remembered by our prospects.

In fact, it's better if one cascades off the other because then you've got common messaging; it's all tied together. Converting an article into a webinar is one example. But you could also create a recorded interview or series of shorter-themed articles to unpack the story a bit more for your audience.

Then, social media posts could help drive traffic to your longer-form content or website. It's a really popular conversion, especially for leaders or executive audiences, to translate a whitepaper that takes some concentration to read, but instead create a 20-30 minute video to highlight some of the main aspects.

The concept is similar to a podcast in that you're getting the insights and the thought process for that company to bring the story to life. Always avoid a hard sell, steer clear of approaches that feel intrusive or overly self-promotional, and instead focus on creating value and building trust.

For example, rather than leading with product features, start by addressing a real challenge your prospect is facing and share insights or solutions that position you and your company as a helpful resource, not just a seller.

Remember, your prospect is already interested. They are reading your paper. They are watching your presentation. They are listening to your podcast. They are watching your video. You already have their attention, and hopefully, your brand is sprinkled throughout. You don't need to be in sales mode here, thinking about closing the deal. Just let your prospect, your reader, absorb the information and get informed to maintain interest.

Variable format and types of content drive impact, too. A blend of quick-hit video and long-form content presents a well-layered approach for helping your market unpack information. The whitepaper fits into the category of what we call long-form content. But it's also helpful for an executive reading about your solution. I know a lot of executives, myself included, who want to catch up on the weekend or during some downtime by going through some of that longer content. On the other side, a blog or simple article can be the middle ground between a longer paper or webinar and a social media post.

Social media posts are going to drive your prospects to longer-form content or get their quick interest to see if this is something they want to learn more about, especially as they're scrolling or it "pops up" in their feed. You want to guide them toward more in-depth content to gauge their interest, explore how it applies to their business, and ultimately invite them to a call or meeting. It involves multiple steps and flows through several channels; that's the essence of multi-channel marketing.

You're never selling just the product but also the services or applications that go with it. That's another way that you can stand out, by having a more holistic view. You might be selling a self-service product or simple service that customers sign up for and don't even go through a salesperson. It could be something that they buy and consume quite easily with e-commerce. Since there isn't a salesperson at this point to guide the customer, a tiered offering is a great way to show different levels for your buyer to self-select based on their needs, price considerations, or length of time (e.g., for a service).

This gives you an idea about how to formulate a strategy based on different formats and types of content. As I mentioned before, this is why you're not going to just dive into the content and, like chasing a squirrel, run after what's popular. It depends on *who* you're trying to reach, *how* you're trying to reach them, and what formats they prefer, so you don't get overloaded trying to do all of it. It's going to be very strategic and intentional.

It's also important to keep it simple and get to the point. Even if you're using long-form content, you are still making points and helping your reader consume it. Earlier, we discussed avoiding corporate jargon, especially in messaging. Include a healthy mix of relevant industry words. **Be careful not to win the keyword battle but lose customer interest.** This can happen if the material is stuffed with all the right words, but your concepts are not understood because the customer cannot understand what you're saying.

One way to counter this is to step back and reread the material. Does it pass the clarity test? In other words, could you explain it to someone outside your field, such as a parent, a student, or a new colleague?

That would not be necessary for a more technical audience, but the content still has to be factual and easy to understand for that prospect.

> *"Why does your audience have to unpack and look up terms or try to understand what you're saying? The answer is they won't unpack your message."*

They will go somewhere else. We want to take away all those friction points. Communication is tapping into the heart and mind. To that point, you are reaching the heart and mind of your audience through your message. Your brand begins to emerge and connect with your market. Your message will have a consistent "flavor," and there's a consistent feel to your brand.

Remember, we really want to make sure that your customer feels heard and that you hear them. You want them to see your messaging and think, *Ah, they understand my problem. They get me.*

Just think of yourself in that space, whether it's in the professional B2B world or as a consumer. How many times have you seen either an ad or a post and thought, *I have to have that*, or *This company gets me?* It's so clear when a company operates in that space.

When we say "hearts and minds," this doesn't mean it all has to be qualitative. Stats are a really great way to confirm and show understanding of the problem statement. I have worked with clients where we've created messaging to show [X]% time savings or [X]% efficiency. This is especially important if you are working in a tech field, such as software, automation, or AI.

Scenario

I have worked with several companies in the tech space over the years to quantify stats and savings. For example, a tech company could say, "On average, across multiple industries, we can provide 25%–30% time savings with our solution." This gives prospective customers an idea of what they could expect, backed by data. Of course, there are disclaimers; the results will rely on other factors such as implementation, expertise, and workflow. But the stats do show that, on average, this was what you could expect. It gives the prospective customer base an idea of where they might fit in, and that is really important for their companies. In fact, I can think of several companies that use a similar formula to quantify the benefits without disclosing any confidential information. Providers typically share aggregate or average data, which the end market finds more useful.

I have also seen other major benefits from automation across industries, such as greater quality and reduced errors from reducing manual entry. Another example is better data management, a single source of information, sometimes called a "single source of truth," and better visibility of the data from all different departments and leaders. Think of it as better "version control" of the data by having proper data governance.

The stats that all of these companies quoted were then used in ads, brochures, websites, presentations, social media, and as a hook in emails. The idea was to provide a specific stat to make the benefits quantifiable and then use it consistently across the marketing materials.

> Tip *Pro tip: Back every benefit or claim with clear, verifiable data to maintain credibility and build trust.*

Even without revealing specific customer data due to privacy constraints, you need to ensure the metric is credible, the supporting data is available, and the entire team understands how the numbers were calculated.

Less is More

Another area to explore in messaging is being aware that there can be too much of a good thing, and too many messages can dilute your story. The classic saying "less is more" applies here. Marketing and sales are excited to talk about brands, products, and services. But sometimes, marketing and sales teams face the challenge of managing a high volume of content across multiple channels. And the last thing you want is to flood the market or leave an interested customer feeling overwhelmed.

Your teams may be struggling with that, and as a leader, you might be thinking, *Why can't we send all of these materials out?* People often underestimate and underinvest in what it takes to get some of these assets put together with quality: social media, blogs, ads, papers, presentations, email cadences, website copy, updates, responses to clients, internal communications, and even if using AI. I think it's simply human nature that we underestimate the time and investment that it takes to create that, not to mention the coordination, alignment, making sure it's all consistent, updates, comparisons to competition, and what else is out there, feedback from customers, proofreading it, and getting stakeholder buy-in.

Intentional marketing shifts the focus from volume of information to targeted and connected across channels.

Shift to intentional marketing

Overload, disconnected ⟹ Targeted, connected

VS

Tactical treadmill | Strategic & measured

It's a lot, but it's never been easier to have a plan, repurpose that content across channels, coordinate, and measure what's coming in from the outside and what your prospects, channel, and market think of your offer and brand. That's why I keep coming back to select a few messages or offers: Get it right, do it well, and build on that; rinse and repeat. That will go much further than trying to just do everything at once. Of course, using tools is powerful and helpful, but be sure to have the strategy aligned first before automating. Automation speeds up and simplifies what is already in place.

When you have that foundation, repurposing is really going to be your secret. The same message is also important. Have you ever noticed that the most powerful brands have a consistent message or graphic treatment across their platforms? Think of McDonald's, AWS, or Microsoft. They all have consistent looks, graphics, messages, and even music. This consistency reinforces the message and builds on recognition. People know what to expect because they see your brand show up so many different times.

This is true for B2B as well, not only for consumers. That's why a multi-channel approach is necessary, such as participating in trade shows and then "showing up" on email and social media. Each person consumes information differently, but having that reinforcement is a critical part of both marketing and sales.

I work with clients all the time on creating a messaging matrix. A matrix is basically a way to map all of their key messages to personas and industry segments. And, it's easy for team members to update, collaborate, and build on as more insights are gained from exchanges with customers. Once you lay it out, you realize: *We don't want to have multiple messages for different channels; we need to appear consistently.* It can be a challenge to scale consistent messaging across a company, and even harder to get everyone aligned. That's when teams start moving in different directions, often reinventing the corporate message due to a lack of clarity or shared understanding. I help clients bring that alignment back, working with them to define and anchor their core messages strategically.

I also think it's important to list the short version of the message versus the long version for your teams. It's always interesting to think about the quick taglines or catchy ads. We all usually want to jump to that, but if you think about it, that's only one form of messaging. That's your quick hit on a scroll in an ad, but you still need longer messages with more depth. That also works really well for SEO (Search Engine Optimization), having that "long tail," such as a phrase that a prospect may look up in a search.

Keep your message clear. If you had a couple of sentences or even a paragraph, what would that look like as a message? It could even be an "elevator pitch" where, if you only had a few minutes with somebody to get from the bottom floor up to a high-rise top floor, what would you say? You want to have that elevator pitch ready to go. It shouldn't sound canned, either. The point is to be able to explain your brand, company, product, and message in a short amount of time and be able to collect that into one area.

This messaging matrix will have short and long forms of claims, messages, and stats. It's always aligned with your ideal customer profile and persona within each ideal customer profile, reducing the risks of teams having different messages. When you make it easy for teams to communicate clearly, you help prospects and clients understand your message without confusion and spark their interest to learn more and start a conversation.

On the other end of the spectrum is a script. It's interesting because, often, companies are criticized for having a script, for literally sounding "too scripted!" This goes back to the issue of corporate jargon. Everything sounds really smooth; too smooth, not human or authentic. In fact, because so many companies in the industry are using similar words, the message is not differentiated but becomes a "sea of sameness."

There's definitely a greater need than ever for a level of authenticity and human speak, a natural and real approach that conveys trust. I see this coming up more and more, especially as we've developed more bots, automation, and AI. Technology is important and powerful, especially when used to enhance our lives and provide true breakthroughs in medicine, economics, living conditions, and opportunity. There is only going to be more need for that in the future. Of course we don't want our brands to sound robotic or buzzword jargon. But then, this doesn't mean that we want our tone of voice to be casual, either. Regardless of the technology, the algorithm, or the brand guide, you should ultimately make sure your message is understandable and doesn't sound scripted or like every other company. It can still be polished and professional, but it must sound authentic.

That's where this matrix will help you, so that it doesn't sound contrived or robotic but aligns messaging across an organization or with partners. And, isn't it interesting and ironic that the bots are now trying to sound more human! We'll cover more in the chapter on technology, but consider the human side of connection and relationships as you craft your messaging.

Test Your Messaging

How can you test your message to make sure that it is resonating? One of the best ways is simply asking people! Ask your prospects, your ideal customers, for feedback. I recommend starting with qualitative, to get a feel or direction. To accomplish this at scale, it's important to use a quantitative approach. This could be a small survey, for example. Another approach that uses specific tools is called A/B testing. It's actually quite simple: testing two different concepts and isolating a change. In fact, we make similar decisions all the time without realizing it, such as choosing a clever theme for an event and asking for feedback, or selecting a powerful tagline or image for a brand. The goal is to measure feedback and adjust course. Advertisers price their space based on reactions. As a business leader, you also need to know exactly the performance of your investments.

Market feedback is one of the most important elements in business. Technology is changing so quickly, and we have the opportunity to adapt *with* it and use the tools to gain data-driven insights. When it comes to doing this with digital, this could be ads, or it could be emails that you're setting up. You might have heard the term "dial in your marketing for impact." The most important thing, though, is that you'll want to change just one thing because if you have two completely separate ads, you don't really know which part resonated and which didn't.

We are investing in marketing, and our brand reputation is being formed with each message. With so many tools collecting data, this is an important way to use data-driven insights to improve messaging. But don't let AI tell your story; instead, use AI to help you tell the story to get the best of both. AI can help navigate through the chaos and get to the right person, but human relationships and problems being solved are what build business.

If you think about it, you are isolating one part of what you're trying to test to figure out what's working. I like the term "dial in your marketing for impact" because it means you're constantly refining it. We are using the popular concept of Agile, basically making iterations and continuous changes, and tweaks.

These techniques are great ways to get precise information for the most impact. However, it surprises me how many marketing teams and companies skip some of these steps for customer feedback, even when the tools are embedded in the platforms. It's definitely something that you'll want to do in different ways.

The difference is that the question needs to be posed with your ideal customer base because you want to make sure you're getting feedback from the applicable group, the voices that matter. Another important aspect is validating that you are solving the problems that matter to the person you are marketing to, or the persona. The messaging and treatment are not only about testing the words and imagery, but ensuring this hits the mark. Some common pitfalls include:

- Too generic of a message, casting a wide net that doesn't resonate with those you want to reach
- Sounds the same as other companies, customers can't really see the difference
- What do you do? If a prospect can't quickly see what you do, they'll move on.

Some of these might sound basic, but they are easy traps to fall into as companies try for the perfect wording that quickly becomes jargon or is too bland.

There are different ways to get feedback, such as changing some of the key wording or tagline. For comparison, maybe one message is very quantitative, talking about the 15% cost savings, while the other one is more about customer satisfaction. By keeping everything else the same, we're testing the benefit statement to see which one's more compelling and which problem is now being solved. Maybe they both come out well, and now you've got two different options. At this stage, we're trying to see what the reaction will be, especially before spending a lot of money in each of these areas.

Be sure to track the results and make informed adjustments. Sometimes teams run tests but don't take the time to review the data, missing a key opportunity to improve performance.

Top tip: Create your tagline to get perspective.

Tip

Creating a tagline or brand statement can help keep your value to your customers clear. I work with companies on defining their value and offers and how to communicate that in a way that resonates. Creating a compelling tagline isn't easy, but it's something nearly everyone thinks about. Even if you don't plan to commercialize it right away, identifying a phrase you're truly proud of creates meaning and understanding. The statement provides a clear foundation for customers to quickly understand.

A strong starting point is to begin at the top level, similar to the approach discussed in the previous chapter regarding the structure and content of a potential press release. The same concept with messaging: what does your tagline look like, sound like? A short phrase can help rally around the right concept. This is a great setup for how we use both positioning and messaging to go out into the market with our story, part of our go-to-market approach.

CHAPTER 4

LET'S GO TO MARKET

Strategy into High-Performing Channel Execution

After sharpening your marketing focus, positioning the brand, product, or service, and working out the messaging, it's now time to activate your go-to-market plan. This next phase is about selecting the right pathways or GTM motions, such as inbound, outbound, events, product-led, service-led, community, ABM, or partner, to reach your next customers effectively and efficiently. In this chapter, we'll explore how to evaluate and execute GTM motions that reflect your business model, sales strategy, and market dynamics. Once the appropriate GTM motions are strategically determined, the messaging can be refined to fully align and be tailored to the expectations of that audience. High-performing channel execution isn't about being everywhere; it's about being in the right places with purpose and intention.

GTM Partners is a well-known research company in this space with a strong GTM Operating System (OS). They bring together a common approach to the wider GTM transformation. They work with high-growth companies to help them unify their GTM teams through frameworks. The channels or GTM motions are a key part of this transformation.

In the introduction, I quoted GTM Partners: "GTM is a transformational process for accelerating your path to market, with high-performing revenue teams delivering a connected customer experience." Here, we connect the strategy with the execution and specific channels.

According to Gartner, a leading global research and advisory firm, "A go-to-market (GTM) strategy is a plan that details how an organization can engage with customers to convince them to buy their product or service and to gain a competitive advantage. A GTM strategy includes tactics related to pricing, sales, and channels, the buying journey, new product or service launches, product rebranding, or product introduction to a new market."[11]

Keep the formula simple: you have a product, service, or offering for customers. Now you need to find them. A few questions you can ask yourself:

- Where do your ideal customers spend their time learning and gathering information?

- Where do your prospects or ideal customers (personas) go to get information and learn about the industry or new solutions?

Having a balanced view on both will help you expand your thinking while staying true to what is working with your current, loyal customer base.

---

[11] Gartner, "Go-to-Market (GTM) Strategy," *Gartner*, accessed 2025, https://www.gartner.com/en/sales/glossary/go-to-market-gtm-strategy.

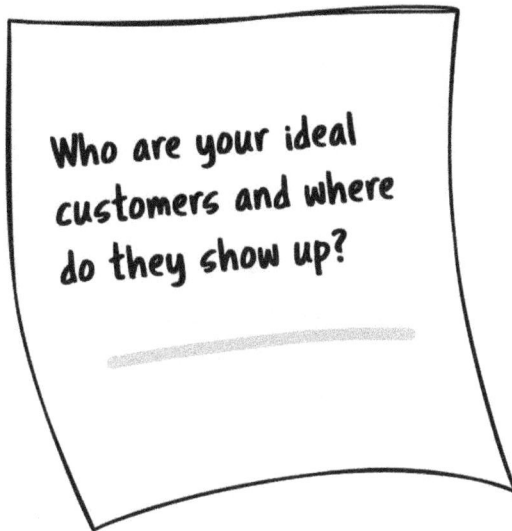

Who are your ideal customers and where do they show up?

It's simple to understand as a consumer: if you need groceries, you will find them in a physical grocery store or an online store. If you are looking for clothes, you will find them at any number of physical retail or online stores. It really is the same thing for commercial or B2B. The art is to work out where they "show up," whether digitally, in person, or both, as you think about your channel and GTM approach.

What's important to the customer will drive where they show up. For example, B2B buyers looking for an automated software platform to help streamline operations in HR or accounting could use a mix of online search and specific industry organizations. These potential customers may look for face-to-face industry events or online webinars to address specific topics.

Connecting Through Problem Solving

First, we discussed identifying the types of problems you help solve. What level of pain or market demand does your solution address? Then we looked at what the willingness to pay is from your ideal customer. Next, we asked, "How big is this problem?" to look at market size. We then looked at *who* has these problems, or the **persona**. We analyzed how to best position your product or service with respect to the competition to make it clear to your market. Then we moved into how you can most effectively communicate and message to the market so that your value proposition and offering can truly resonate and be understood.

At this point, we're ready to get out into the market and connect through our marketing strategies and plan. We want to look at how to reach our market with powerful tools and understanding. Depending on where your ideal customer can be found, it's going to be more than one place. For example, think about industry associations with leaders, online forums in social media for specific industries, email, and specific events.

Selecting a Primary GTM Approach

We know that buying teams will need to consume information from multiple channels, from reading reviews to researching solutions to possibly talking to other peers for perspective. We also know they will need to see the information multiple times to be remembered and resonate.

Tip *An important tip: Decide on the primary or core marketing channel where you're going to start.*

This will certainly be different for consumer goods versus B2B, and even for a specialized niche. We see companies trying hard to differentiate and claim a niche, or small part of a larger segment, for that specialization. Even this approach needs to be taken into account in the go-to-market strategy.

In consumer goods, a company may spend heavily on brand and mass markets, such as social media and maybe even television and internet ads. In many cases, they are casting a wider net to reach a larger base. For them, it's about volume and reaching many people with a consistent message. The transaction might even be done through a distribution-type channel without directly involving the core company.

Procter & Gamble, or P&G, is a recognized expert in consumer goods. Often, their messaging makes their product memorable. P&G is also a true leader in consumer brand management. They are known for managing multiple brands under one umbrella, their brand architecture.[12]

If you are in B2B, you are probably in awe of some of the characteristics of consumers. I'm amazed that some of the consumer brands have enjoyed the same brand character and concept for decades. Even though we know a significant investment goes into the brand, it's a positive sign that the manufacturer didn't feel the need to rebrand and bring in a new character every year.

Companies such as Kellogg's have created a timeless concept that lasts generations. They clearly understand their family-focused market and aim to build products that span decades. They have the ability to change other elements around it and refresh or update. For a company such as Kellogg's, family around the breakfast table is definitely part of their brand. The same character on the cereal box year after year continues to build instant recognition and familiarity, a consistent branding tool across generations. Of course, they are spending a lot of money on branding and GTM, but this demonstrates an important lesson on keeping elements in place that are working and providing continuity and consistency.

What is that equivalent in B2B? We want to create a connection, a consistent concept that transcends a given ad, email, or event. One example is for a local law firm to create an image of trust, such as articulating that they have been around for decades and will continue to serve the community. Another

---

[12] The Brand Hopper, "Understanding the Brand Architecture of Procter & Gamble (P&G)," *The Brand Hopper*, accessed March 2025, https://thebrandhopper.com/2023/07/13/understanding-the-brand-architecture-of-proctor-gamble-pg/.

example is serial entrepreneurs launching under a new brand but leveraging years of experience, with technology integrated in a new way.

How do you reach your ideal customers? Consider where they go and what information they need. That's why I keep coming back to how important it is not to jump at everything you hear or see in one market. It might not be the best spend of your marketing investment for an expensive influencer campaign if your market prefers a more technical whitepaper or F2F meeting.

It goes back to that squirrel analogy. Not everyone needs to have daily video posts. Perhaps it's LinkedIn for your brand or a series of highly credible industry articles. The reason you'll want to select a primary channel is that it gives your company an anchor and a way to compare investments and return on investment among channels. Which strategies and channels are moving the needle?

GTM Motions

There are a number of different channels and ways to approach your marketing through a coordinated effort across marketing, sales, and customer functions. **Your GTM strategy defines** *where you're going, who you're targeting,* **and** *why customers should care.* Marketing channels, whether it's executive meetings, email, webinars, direct messages, paid ads, social media, or trade shows, are simply how you get there. Choosing the right ones depends on understanding your market, message, and customer journey.

For alternatives, let's look at some of the most popular go-to-market motions. These can really vary by type, method, and medium, as well as the cost necessary in terms of time, resources, and pure spend. We're also going to cover several different types of go-to-market motions.

Outbound: Reaching Out to Drive Interest

Let's start with "outbound." This GTM motion involves reaching out to your market and making contact. Too often, marketing is associated with pure outreach. We know that marketing is much broader and that each type of GTM motion has its purpose and strength. Outbound is very common, one of the most common forms.

One of the most important reasons for the outbound approach is to have a steady stream of interest and leads. Think of it as "always-on" communication to prospective buyers, which works in parallel to your other GTM efforts, which we'll cover. You never know when your prospect will open the right email or receive the right message that resonates. And one of the most important aspects is to recognize that not everyone is ready to buy now. In fact, only 5% are estimated to be in the market for your product or service on average at a given moment.[13] You can calculate this based on how often a customer may need your product or service, and it varies by industry. But the 5%–7% rule has been fairly widely adopted. This might sound obvious, but many marketers will interpret a response as an interest to buy. In fact, the interest can often be the initial research that your prospect is starting.

You have probably heard or used the term "cold call." It may conjure up negative feelings of spammy, aggressive phone calls, emails, or even website pop-ups. Unfortunately, overly aggressive tactics have given the term a bad name and reputation. However, when cold outreach is done properly, and you send the right message, it's going to pique interest.

The reason it is called "cold" is not because it's supposed to be aggressive! We call it "cold" because the prospect likely has not been contacted before, and this could be the initial connection. The lead will need to be "warmed

---

[13] Frank Strong, "Only 5% of B2B Buyers Are in Market Today; But Where Did That Statistic Come From?," *Sword and the Script*, April 2024, https://www.swordandthescript.com/2024/04/5-percent-b2b-buyers/.

up" through exchanging information and interaction. You have likely heard of the opposite extreme, "hot lead," which is a buyer perceived to be both interested and ready to buy.

For cold outreach, we reach out to new prospects with clever messaging that aligns with your company and solution's positioning. The messaging has been crafted to reach the ideal customer and a specific person in the role (persona). The prospect may view it as "spam," but that could also indicate that they're not really the right target, as they are not interested in *this* solution at *this* time.

Let's unpack the scenario where this prospect is the right type of company and the right role/persona, but is not ready to buy now. In this case, we want to continue to stay top of mind and keep your company on their "radar" without being annoying. In marketing, we can create a "nurture campaign" to maintain the customer's interest. It's optimal to share information about the industry, changes you're seeing, and educational snippets. You can certainly share any new products, services, or innovations to capture their attention. Another approach is to offer a special or something seasonal.

Many companies will acknowledge holidays or industry events as a way to stay connected. The key is to be authentic. The goal is to stay top of mind and be ready to interact when the time is right. You could write an interesting article to keep the ball in play. Think about emails that you have received from companies. You might stay subscribed in case you need that type of service, or you find the content interesting. In these cases, the company sending you these emails is trying to keep its brand known. And that's what a nurture campaign can accomplish, to literally nurture the relationship and communications.

Another common mistake with outbound messages is sending very generic messages to prospects. It doesn't actually "speak" to them. In contrast, one of the best ways to keep prospects interested is to personalize the message and make the focus more about them. How do you solve their problems? Get inside their world. Too often, we see examples of emails or social posts all about the company, excited about its own product or service, and capabilities. To make content more relevant to your prospects, share ideas, educate them on industry changes, or new information through emails.

Here is an example: a data management company shares an article about the latest issues in cybersecurity and strategies to protect. In the next article or email, the same company shares helpful information about new regulations on data privacy. A startup in healthcare offering a remote monitoring device shares a piece on early warning signs for chronic diseases, including specific stats on the benefits of monitoring. The company is connecting with the prospect on the topic, and less about their solution at this point. They provide links to articles, website pages, offers, and videos; it's a more subtle opportunity to connect.

When organizations haven't implemented ongoing outreach or communication efforts, they are limited to reaching only the audiences currently targeted by their ads or social media, and they lack a consistent methodology. That's where a customer relationship management (CRM) system can help keep track of contacts, engagement, and stats on what has been opened to allow you to more closely understand your market response. That's one method of outbound.

Calls and texts are another. Texts and SMS messages are very popular, even for B2B. SMS has been around for decades, but it's become more acceptable now to use it for outreach. Communicating with a chatbot is another form of exchange. And now bots have moved into outreach, whether for voice communications or to get meetings set up. But whether it's calls or emails, you still want to focus on the problems that you're solving. AI is moving quickly and taking on more of the functions. The real formula is to keep the human spirit in your interactions and leave the automation to *get to* the conversation to AI and the bots.

At this point, our objective is to determine whether this prospect fits the ideal customer profile. If they do not, it actually saves us time and money to move on. It's better to know that, so you're not wasting your effort. In a B2B context, the goal in your calls is to engage and qualify, and then move them to the next call and provide them with more information. Don't try to overload them or accomplish everything in one call or email. Simply test out if the information is of interest to them. You don't want to put pressure on them. Your goal should be for the long term, not a quick hit or a quick sale; it should never be a quick hit or sale. You're building a relationship.

Advertising is the next format of outbound and applies to all markets, whether consumer, government, or B2B. This is a great place to think about where your ideal customer receives their information. Digital ads are extremely popular and effective. Local businesses rely on geographically targeted digital ads, social media promotions, and print advertisements. B2B companies specialize more in social media platforms, industry events and associations, and sponsored/syndicated content on curated platforms and websites. There are so many media options to consider, such as print, digital platforms, social media ads, television, industry events, and radio.

For advertising, you could be offering a special promotion, announcing a new product or service, or simply bringing visibility to your brand. The point is that you are connecting with your market with a call to action on something of interest, where you are looking for a response.

We always want to measure the response to our marketing efforts. The goal is to view what is most effective and then adjust course with your investments. Here is another great opportunity for A/B testing to compare emails, copy, ads, to see what's working.

Account-Based Marketing (ABM): A Strategic Outbound GTM Play

Account-based marketing is a very popular and excellent approach to reach specific companies. I have a lot of experience with this approach and have helped companies with their strategy and execution. The goal is to create highly targeted, highly personalized communication to varying stakeholders at different levels of the target company. The concept is for marketing and sales to target specific companies within the ideal customer profile and personalize communications and outreach directly to the key decision-makers within that company, typically in senior leadership roles. The content is customized based on data and insights drawn from the data or knowledge about the company.

We typically use ABM with mid-sized to large enterprises. I have seen many larger companies adopt a personalized, account-based strategy that brings marketing and sales together. This targeted approach drives deeper engagement through personalization and requires a high level of market understanding to succeed. ABM can be tremendously successful given the personalization versus mass market approach.

The goal is to develop a game plan, looking at who's who within the customer base. How can your teams reach each of those prospects? What are the key problems that your company is solving for the target customers? ABM focuses on finding specific individuals at multiple levels in the target account and mapping a plan for their pain points. The best practice is to identify the relationships from your company to the ideal target company and form a contact map.

The next step is a coordinated outbound campaign, tying together messages in emails, social media, and ads. The campaign can be targeted at more than one company, but it needs to be targeted and focused to build credibility and trust through personalization. The point of personalization and going deep versus wide continues to be popular and successful.

ABM is a very strategic GTM motion. It is usually used in B2B with a specific scope and investment, which can vary depending on the amount of activity, personalization, and channels. The goal, of course, is conversion and moving the decision-makers to buy.

Inbound: Leads/Prospects Coming to You

"Inbound" is one of the most popular types of GTM motions. The name even implies that potential customers are seeking your company out. Inbound is a longer game but benefits from the "fatigue" and even distaste prospects have from overly aggressive marketers who have done high volume outbound or perceived spam. We are all getting hit from these different directions.

The name implies interest coming in, but these leads or prospective buyers didn't just magically appear. Companies invest in content such as brochures, videos, and articles to attract customers' attention. The prospective buyer has expressed interest, or what we call "intent," meaning they have intention toward your company. Most likely, they are coming to your company based on interacting with one of the marketing and sales assets put out there, such as the website, an eBook, or a "top five ways" guide. For example, an engineering manager is researching companies with secure cloud services and has downloaded a whitepaper. The "lead" now comes into the company's CRM as an "inbound" lead.

In the example of a downloaded white paper, the content may have resonated with the prospect. Another example would be a social media post or blog article that the company posted could have prompted a COO to click a link and reach out for more information or to schedule a call. Let's face it, you've spent a lot of money, effort, and thought to create and place these materials. We want to measure the response; it's important to see the return on having these leads come into your funnel. On inbound, you've made organic materials available to your market and prospects to prompt a response of interest.

Potential clients are showing interest by requesting more information or engaging with content through downloads. SEO may be contributing to this interest by surfacing the right keywords. The key point is that the market is responding with clear signs of interest, and the brand or content is resonating.

There are significant efforts and investment to make content and websites more easily found through keywords, phrases, compelling images, the right channels, correct positioning and many more elements. The efforts are paying off as inbound leads come in. By understanding the digital marketing system and the algorithm, marketing teams can position the business to better connect with its buyers.

AI makes it possible to do even more now with the go-to-market motions, especially with inbound. For example, most of the digital marketing platforms are integrating AI to drive more personalization and automate time-consuming workflows.

When executed properly, both machine automation and human connection can work together for the best outcome. Let AI and automation focus on the mechanics so you and your team can focus on the human side of connection and nuanced market understanding for the best of both worlds. Most leaders agree that automation today is helping take the manual burden off of teams and letting workers get back to the actual jobs they were hired to do.

Most companies are using a blend of inbound and outbound GTM strategies as their primary methods. One of the most important objectives is to keep your prospects engaged, which we'll cover further in this chapter. Although there are excellent tools to help measure and drive engagement, success starts with a clear strategy.

One important consideration for "inbound" is to review whether these new prospects are within the ideal customer profile. If they are outside of the "persona" you would normally be targeting, then you need to consider if this is a fit or not. The answer will depend on several factors, such as how close the offer will be that you provide, their ability to buy, and whether you will see other customers in this same adjacent area.

If this is a good fit, then there's no need to change your marketing messaging. However, if you are receiving several requests outside of your core ideal customer profile scope, then it could be time to adjust your messaging. Otherwise, you'll spread your efforts too thin and are unlikely to make an impact with your core base.

Product-Led and Service-Led

Next, we'll explore product-led and service-led go-to-market motions. Both of these GTM motions became popular for driving product usage in different parts of the life cycle. Software platforms that scale often have a product-led strategy. The Product Led Alliance provides a definition: "A **product-led go-to-market (GTM) strategy** places the product at the center of every stage of the customer journey. The product itself becomes the primary vehicle for attracting, converting, and retaining users. With product-led GTM, potential customers interact directly with the product, often through freemium models or free trials, allowing them to experience its value before making a purchase decision."[14]

How often have you seen a "free version" or tier of a product, especially a software too. As users experience the product, they may need more advanced capabilities or want to add other team members or clients. Users have the option to upgrade to paid tiers. Some examples in B2B are Canva, Slack, and Zoom. Each of these platforms offer different tiers of the experience, product updates, and messaging all take place within the product platform.

The product-led and service-led GTM motions are very specific and will not apply to every company. This GTM approach is a popular way for some of

---

[14] Rebecca Madro, "What Is Product-Led Go-to-Market (GTM)?," *Product-Led Alliance*, October 11, 2024, https://www.productledalliance.com/mastering-product-led-gtm/.

the software players to be able to reach their market. On the consumer side, think about Spotify or Duolingo in the translation industry. Typically, these platforms have a self-service concept or online help videos. Another popular aspect they incorporate is user communities, so you can share with other users and educate each other.

Service-led is slightly different and builds on expertise and a unique value proposition related to the service. In this GTM motion, there is an opportunity for customization, ongoing engagement to truly prioritize strong relationships, and deliver exceptional service. A few examples include customer support, consulting, or managed services which are the core offering to drive a mix of customer acquisition, satisfaction, and loyalty.

The essence of product-led or service-led is working within your solution and expertise as the platform. This approach provides the advantage of built-in potential for advocacy across the user base, which is powerful. Essentially, users help other users on the platform through the community, not the company driving adoption. The integrated community automatically brings "built-in differentiation" to the brand.

Events

Events are the next GTM strategy and very popular, available in more formats and "flavors" than ever before. Events are exciting because they bring together humans and can go much deeper into core concepts, more holistically across the industry. From a GTM perspective, events can tie together several aspects of marketing and sales.

For example, there are outbound efforts ahead of the event to reach new potential customers and to invite them to the event. There is also an inbound element when customers see the event on the website or through an ad and take action to register. Social media, advertising, and even the press can play an important role. There is a tremendous human connection here, an exchange of information and ideas, thought leadership, and true reflection on the topics. Events can be face-to-face, virtual, or hybrid (a mix of both) and offer an opportunity for depth of content, such as top leadership messaging, subject matter expertise, demos and exhibits, executive meetings, and time for social gatherings, as a few examples.

It's no surprise that events are one of the more expensive GTM investments, and often companies will prioritize and focus on the most relevant for their industry and business objectives. There is a rising trend for mid-sized and larger companies to host their own events, such as Salesforce and its massive event, Dreamforce. The same is happening in smaller niches, too, because it's a way to curate who's coming to the event and have a more tailored agenda and experience.

Companies typically participate in major industry events to position themselves as top players in their field. Often, they will invest in a sponsorship, which provides more prominent exhibition space or a speaking opportunity, for example. Both of these examples are important lead opportunities to bring in new prospects and influence current prospects in the sales funnel. A speaking opportunity raises the profile of the company, provides a credible way to share the story and relate to ideal customers, and builds relationships. The booth or exhibit space provides the prospective customer a unique opportunity to meet directly with subject matter experts and leaders to ask questions, see demos, or learn about services or case studies. Virtual events can offer similar formats with speaking opportunities and virtual meeting rooms for meet and greet or demos.

It's important to pick and choose *which* events are most critical for your company. I always recommend attending an event or seeking a strong recommendation before investing in sponsorship. Remember, for a lot of companies, one of their prime motivations to attend is to network, to meet other companies and build relationships in the industry in addition to promoting their brand or learning about other suppliers.

Participants expect more of an engaging experience and dialogue at events. They invest time, time away from other work, and travel expenses. Here are a few common objectives and goals:

- Understand the latest in the industry, innovation, technology, and key players.
- Meet and interact with new contacts, build relationships.
- Educate themselves at a deeper level, such as demos, talks, and panels.
- Network at informal events.
- Meet with other peers in the industry to compare notes and gain perspective.
- Collect insights to bring back and share with other stakeholders.
- Conduct meetings with customers (or partners).

They want to gain value on their investment to spend the dedicated time and money for the physical event. And, the goal is not only to meet potential suppliers but also to meet other peers in the industry and learn a broader perspective. Where is the industry heading? Several years ago, going to "trade shows" was a way to better understand the companies in the space, and a major trigger for a buying event within the industry.

Trade shows have a massive following and are a powerful way for companies to demonstrate their point of view in a market, where they're headed with their roadmap, and where the industry is going, trends. Companies sometimes save announcements on new releases and new products for these large-scale events. Events offer fantastic opportunities for networking. Often, you will see social events tied in with executive dinners or sponsored events, everything from a happy hour to a cycling event to a lineup of power speakers to draw people into the experience.

The price is high, and the stakes are high as a percentage of the budget. The costs to consider are travel, the opportunity cost of pulling the team out from normal business operations, and pricey sponsor packages. But the ROI is strong and, when done right, can absolutely pay off. The key is to build the prioritized events into your marketing plan and know that it's going to be one of your major go-to-market motions. Consider that there is also a risk and downside competitive threat for not being at an event, and the message this can send to your market.

After participating as a sponsor in an industry event, look holistically at the return on your investment. Consider whether to continue to sponsor at the same level or even increase sponsorship if there is a strong response. You could upgrade to a better exhibit location next year or move from display only to adding a speaking slot for more exposure and to drive foot traffic to the booth. Review the data and analytics from the event for an objective view to gauge performance and assess future participation. Consider the impact on the quality of contacts and the number of conversations that led to further discussions.

Since events can be virtual (online), face-to-face, or a hybrid approach, you can use a mix to reach your audience. For online, multi-day events, it's important to consider what will hold your audience's attention and keep the time manageable. Also, consider offering the links for playback later since many interested participants may not be able to join live. Think about how to differentiate from a simple webinar, such as using a platform that mirrors a physical event. Roundtable discussions and panels offer interesting ways to engage an audience with more interaction and a variety of speakers. Another popular format is a more exclusive dinner or networking event in a particular city. This format reduces costs all around and creates a more intimate experience. You can still have a speaker or offer an opportunity to demo a product, meet the experts, or learn more about your company.

Regardless of the type of event or level of participation, as with all elements of marketing, be sure to review the results and adjust course. The format and style depend on the results you are looking to achieve. Are you introducing a new concept? Commenting on how technology such as AI agents will impact your industry?

> 💡 **Tip** *Tip: Remember that marketing of the event happens before, during, and after.*

For greater impact, leverage other marketing channels ahead, such as email marketing and social media posting, to inform your customers and prospects about your participation at the event. Some of the best practices include "meet us there" or giving the audience a preview of some of the content themes, announcements, or launch information. These tactics will help build credibility and showcase your company as adding value in the industry.

After the event, send follow-ups to thank participants for joining. The follow-up is also an excellent opportunity to provide a recap of key outcomes, learnings, and ideas shared during the event. Always provide a link or CTA (call to action) on where they can learn more or engage with you or your company.

Partnerships and Alliances

Another important GTM play is partnerships and alliances. Given the pace of change and the number of new companies emerging, I believe many companies are refining their partnership approach. Think of a partnership as a collaboration between two or more companies with joint benefits; they each typically bring complementary expertise rather than competitive expertise.

For example, one company might offer a product, while the other provides a service. Another example could involve a smaller company partnering with a larger one that's part of a broader ecosystem with multiple companies under a single umbrella. In these partnerships, sales teams often compare accounts to identify opportunities for collaboration. The goal is to cast a wider net and make more effective use of sales resources and efforts. A smaller company may have a brilliant product or technology but lack the resources to scale through outbound or inbound go-to-market (GTM) plays.

For the larger company, the partnership strengthens their brand by allowing them to offer highly specialized expertise without having to develop it in-house. For the smaller company, it provides scale. Often, the larger partner has an established go-to-market network, such as a national or global sales team, which the smaller company can tap into. This allows the technology company to focus on what it does best while leveraging the larger partner as its go-to-market channel. In this example, the partnership becomes a central component of the smaller company's go-to-market strategy.

One B2B example is technology companies partnering with specialized solution providers to combine platform strength with niche expertise. For example, large tech companies like ServiceNow, Oracle, IBM, Microsoft, Adobe, and Salesforce all have robust partner programs that attract different types of partners. The structure of the partnership can vary depending on expertise. A few examples of these structures include resellers, technology partners, ISVs (independent software vendors), system integrators, consulting/advisory, and many more flavors.

For smaller companies, the primary outreach might be through partners because it's very expensive for these growing companies to try to replicate all of the different go-to-market motions on their own, especially industry events.

Co-branding is very important, too. A typical format is a slide featuring partner logos that showcases the ecosystem of partnering companies and brands. The partnership enables companies to focus on whatever specific aspect of the market or solution they handle. Shopify has offered different incentive programs ranging from flat fees to a percentage of sales. Red Hat is another good example. They built a platform for developers, and they thrive on a combination of partnership and community go-to-market motions.

Community

The Community GTM motion is related to partnership, but has a very distinct format and approach. Community used to be associated with software or "user groups," but is more widely considered a network of power users or affiliates that are using the product or service, and in the best case, are also passionate about the brand. I think the benefits are obvious in terms of brand advocacy and self-driven support. The secret is to get the community right and provide excellence in the same way that companies want to build positive reviews and referrals.

Typically, people feel a sense of connection when they are part of something bigger. In B2B, that can mean engaging with a trusted, unbiased community where participants freely share "best practices," templates, ideas, and perspectives or advice. A great example of building community is Slack. The company has built a product to host communities, so they completely understand how to use that model to gain traction. I believe Slack focused on a core ideal customer profile, which was startups, and also on product teams. They didn't target executives at first; instead, they let the advocacy grow organically, and then teams felt they "had to have this tool."

In the early days, the product was seen as a way to offset the massive email overload. There was a phrase, "Just Slack me" or "I'll watch for it on Slack," shorthand for a type of communication outside of email. The company solved the problem of reducing emails because work was streamlined more efficiently through these community channels. They also introduced a fun, casual tone and positioned themselves with *ease of use*. The problem they were solving was the jammed email inbox and busy workers needing to piece together different threads and conversations, version control, and pure overwhelm.

On the consumer side, I always think of Crumbl Cookies, where users post pictures of their favorite cookies. There are social media groups driving affinity. The company has a clever marketing strategy with the "big reveal" on Sunday night to see the flavors of the week and create a little bit of hype. Part of the community approach includes a cookie journal to document and remember each cookie. I could go on, but the idea is that this brand leverages community right in the community! Cookie customers are collaborating and sharing pictures and updates with their friends. You can send your friend a cookie as a gift. It's a phenomenal example of branding and positive user experience through community.

Another example, and one that has stood the test of time, is LEGO. For their approach, LEGO uses a few different go-to-market strategies, and because of their size and appeal, this makes sense. The brand is definitely well-known for the community they have created. LEGO has a very innovative approach, empowering users to actually co-create new LEGO designs. If a design receives enough votes, the company may even take it into production. That's incredibly powerful for the market. The company has also set up advocate networks, where super users and ambassadors can provide structured feedback to the company. It's yet another way of really listening to their market.

When I think about the B2B side, a lot of companies will have advisory groups, where they get structured feedback and listen to prime users. In all of these cases, one of the main outcomes is driving loyalty and strong advocacy through a successful product or service line. The advisory group is not focused on direct selling but instead on a higher level of engagement and experience.

Companies need to be careful though, with this community concept. Remember, if your customer base isn't happy, if your community isn't happy, that sentiment will spread. Ensure your company is performing and delivering and leverage the community to help through insights, then act on improvements and demonstrate continuous listening and action.

Bringing Together the GTM Motions

Here is a table of the GTM motions that we covered:

Popular GTM Motions	Attributes
Outbound	Form new connections, cast a wider net, personalized outreach at scale
Inbound	Coming to you based on something you "put out there," such as content or a website
Product led	Self-serve and user-driven; product drives acquisition, usage, and expansion
Service led	Expertise-driven, high-touch; builds on relationships and a personalized approach
Events	F2F or virtual; engagement-driven and experiential; relationship building
Partnerships/Alliances	Complementary skills to scale, such as technology, commercial, service, or market access
Community	Advocacy and peer-driven, high degree of knowledge sharing and organic growth
ABM (Account-Based Marketing)	High touch, ultra-personalized for high-value accounts; tends to be executive-focused, can be part of 'outbound'.
Other	There are several others, including customer-led (e.g referrals), ecosystem, and influencer-led

Most companies use several GTM motions, not only one. Problems occur when companies try to employ all or "as many as possible" without a clear strategy. This is expensive and also wastes resources by not necessarily reaching the ideal customer profile.

Scenario

Here is a specific case study to help articulate the points and make them more real. I worked with several companies in the tech space whose teams were mostly focused on inbound. The conversion was phenomenal, but the outbound activity within the team was minimal.

In some cases, the inside sales team had limited product training. They had a lack of product knowledge, which meant limited confidence in being able to communicate the value proposition beyond the website. In other companies, there was such a strong inbound pipeline that the "muscle" wasn't built for outbound. The next step was to add outbound to the mix. If you are looking to strengthen your teams' outbound muscle, here are ways you can tackle this in three steps:

1. Invest in **sales enablement**, establishing a training plan and cadence so that the sales team is gaining a deeper understanding of product or service knowledge and can understand the key points including demos.

2. Establish a **hiring plan** to bring in different levels and provide mentoring so the team has greater bench strength to scale. With this tiered model, there is a natural learning for each person to be more successful.

3. Create **consistent talking points** about the core solutions and, more importantly, questions to ask the prospects. This should not need to be a robotic script.

It's a great example of being able to start with one go-to-market motion, add another, and then build from there.

Factors to Consider

You might be asking, "What influences my go-to-market plan?" Consider ROI and budget as two important factors for GTM planning. How much are you spending? That's your budget. What is your allocation, and are you seeing a strong ROI? What investment is required for each motion? What results have you seen? For a low-performing area, can the results be turned around? Simply put, look at what's working and what's not to inform the next steps for GTM planning.

Next, review each channel where your company is interacting with your customer base. The goal is quality relationships, not quantity clicks and hits. Look at the stats across the channels where a prospect has engaged with different sources, such as clicked on an ad, joined a webinar, downloaded an eBook, or commented on a LinkedIn post. These actions on "intent" will help prioritize. With a proper CRM system, reviewing "opportunities" in the funnel based on the "lead scoring" gives a strong indication of which GTM motions and content assets are converting. A lead scoring system will enable you and your team to create your own formula for the types of actions most critical to show intent to buy or at least intent to move to the next stage. In reviewing the stats, identify what is working, what is not converting, and where some adjustments to the message, the action requested, or the channel could make a difference.

What's the best route for your business when it comes to relationship building and networking? For specific industries, such as healthcare or manufacturing, an industry association could bring good visibility to your brand. Keep in mind that it will also bring visibility to your competitors, but it may be where your prospects turn for trusted advice. Another angle would be a technology-based group, such as a standards organization with a common mission or a group focused on AI agent applications.

Certain businesses, such as direct-to-consumer or online e-commerce, may be looking for a more mass-market approach through widespread advertising. Consider whether you are serving a specialized niche. If your market is looking for specific knowledge or a trusted advisor, then maybe a networking group or association is a better fit.

To recap, start by identifying where you can build a strong connection to your market. Map out multi-channel scenarios and model the investment and ROI expectations. Be clear on the impact needed to justify the expenditure. Always remember the long game and consistent growth. Since not everyone is ready to buy, you will want to factor that into your plans. The stat that's most often used is that 5% are ready to buy now.[15] Your job is to stay top of mind without bothering them or scaring them away. Professor Dawes, who wrote about this concept, noted about those not ready, "The 95% figure is not meant to be a precise rule. We're using it as a heuristic to get the idea across that the vast majority of businesses, for a large proportion of products, are not in the market in particular time periods."

Automation through a campaign will help create a steady cadence of communication based on an informative approach. The goal will be to keep your prospect's interest through emails and posts to let them know you are here for them. Think about the brands you interact with that you like and appreciate. You probably don't really think about that company much, but the emails and communication will help you remember: *There is a company that does that service.* When the time is right, you will have a reference point.

---

[15] John Dawes, "The 95:5 Rule," *John Dawes*, accessed June 4, 2025, https://johndawes.info/the-955-rule/.

Avoid too much talk about yourself, your product, and your brand in these informative, ongoing communications. A company can foster a better relationship through a more informative approach such as providing an industry update, educational resource, or a report on changes to policy that impacts the industry. The communications could announce upcoming events, share educational topics, or spotlight relevant news, all of which are important to their business.

I recommend sharing your ideas and best practices on topics such as leadership because most companies want to hear ideas on what they can do differently and learn from experts. Another good category you can cover is "what has changed," the year/s ahead, and the year/s in reflection. Remember: it's not about you; it's about your customer. The information will help you to think about things from their perspective, from their lens. What can they learn? How can you help them? What's their pain point or challenge that is unresolved?

Staying Top of Mind

Once you have the leads mechanism established and you are actively receiving leads, you need to keep the connection. Here are a few examples of ways to stay engaged, focusing on a blend of human connection and automation to simplify the process:

- Sequenced emails and text messages, called "drip campaigns." This could be a time-based series of messages to stay top of mind.

- Response-based messages, called "nurture campaigns." These are often immediate emails, SMS messages, or calls following an action, such as downloading a paper or clicking on a call-to-action (CTA) button.

The goal is to keep the dialogue and mutual interest on the topic and avoid a hard sell. Think of the interaction as an exchange, like volleyball. The ball is going back and forth. You simply want to stay in the game until they are ready. Each article or engagement will also include a CTA. Examples include "schedule a meeting," "book a demo," or "learn more here."

Always give your customers or prospects a way to unsubscribe, too. This not only addresses legal and data privacy needs, but also avoids wasting time and effort where there isn't a fit. The campaign with outreach, such as a periodic email or newsletter, will keep you in the game and top of mind.

Tip: Identify the top two go-to-market strategy **Tip** *approaches that work today for your business.*

Consider your ideal customer profile, how, and where they buy. I work with companies all the time to help build that out and take it to the next level. This quick and easy tip that you can do today will help you with a foundational starting point. From there, you can assess if additional GTM motions are needed to reach your market. Remember, focus on reaching out and resonating with your market.

CHAPTER 5

IT'S ABOUT THE PEOPLE

Relationships Drive Business

We've talked about the different parts of marketing and how you will reach your market. The best strategies start with understanding the people you serve and what's important to them.

Strong relationships drive business growth and build trust. A relationship here means the customer is interacting with you and your company, with your brand. They are getting to know what type of company or person they are engaging with, and are shifting from cold outreach into a much more trusted relationship. The communications will feel personalized and resonate with them.

Trust builds relationships

In fact, referrals and reviews depend on trust. Prospects want to hear from someone who has already purchased the product or service and moved past the initial steps. Another professional vetted and can vouch for this person or this business. In these cases, we accelerate the process to share more with a prospect so they can get to know us. Many prospects will ask for referrals because they want to work with someone who has already been vetted. The vetting can either be through someone they trust or by seeing "enough evidence" in quality reviews.

Ironically, overreliance on reviews can create a blind spot and cause prospects to miss out on real opportunities. Sellers create similar blind spots if they only include prospects who come in through referrals, since it limits the number of potential prospects or clients. A robust marketing and GTM strategy and plan casts a wider net. When you help prospects get to know your company, you make it easier for them to build on the reviews and referrals.

Video also compresses the time it takes to get to know a company by seeing and hearing from the people who represent the brand, the human connection. In summary, reviews, references, speaking to people who have used the product or service, demos, and videos help someone unfamiliar with the company get to know us faster.

Marketing efforts lay the groundwork to let prospects know who you are and what you provide. Now you can have a more focused conversation on something more specific to solve their problems and their business forward.

A nurture campaign further builds the relationship by delivering relevant content that aligns with the stage the prospect is in on their journey. Sharing resources such as presentations, whitepapers, demo videos, and testimonials helps demonstrate your credibility, build trust, and show that you truly understand their business and challenges.

We always want to build relationships with people we haven't met and bring them into the exchange. Most of my clients want to use the connections and relationships they have built as a springboard for new business, whether directly or through a referral.

Many companies use video to help accelerate the time it takes to get to know a prospect. Think about this: when you can see someone speak, hear their message, and understand their perspective, you are more likely to engage in a meeting or explore a business relationship.

That's why webinars and podcasts are so popular and effective; they go deeper and help prospects get to know you. The goal is to open the door to further conversation and engagement.

Authenticity in an Automated, Busy World

Most companies genuinely want to provide outstanding service, build a strong reputation, and attract a steady stream of business. Authenticity resonates with the market. *I believe the human brain holds the ultimate algorithm.* We can line up different systems and keywords to get the best scores in the algorithm, but in the end, it will likely come down to what the human mind thinks and what someone experiences; thus, the term "winning hearts and minds."

Social media overflows with quick tips and brief email advice. Some "experts" will make large claims, the digital version of the shortcut. But in the end, you will gain more long-term business, followers, customers, and expansion through consistent, authentic efforts over quick-hit schemes.

I have worked with companies to focus on themes and campaigns that truly resonated with their market, ranging from bold thought-leadership initiatives to targeted performance metrics such as increasing email engagement, driving up response rates, and improving discoverability in search.

I've helped companies stand out in their market by sharpening their positioning, messaging, and clarifying what they stand for, and how they solve real problems. The clarity leads to better visibility, stronger engagement, and higher rankings. We didn't simply chase algorithms but focused on what resonates with customers. In several cases, I helped companies get to the top page of searches, expand inbound calls, and grow their pipeline.

One of the key themes I work with companies on is consistency. I recommend regular outreach to prospects in human conversation, whether by email, text, or social media. For example, on social media, post consistently, such as three times a week, versus every day, and then nothing. The market and the algorithm will reward you for the regular messaging and cadence. I suggest creating a schedule you can meet and sticking with that plan. Deliver a well-crafted, consistent message to your ideal customer profile, which speaks to the right "persona" and resonates.

More than ever, there's a lot of noise out there with so many platforms and channels. Ironically, one person's "noise" is another person's outbound campaign if not done properly! In the end, everyone's trying to be seen and heard. This is especially true now with AI, which is simplifying and automating the ability to reach markets. AI helps us refine our outreach to be more personalized. We are landing our messages more accurately and to the right inboxes and radars, which will have a greater positive impact.

Companies put off potential customers when there is too much. Too many emails, too quick on the call for action, too assumptive. Go for authenticity. We want our buyer to hear us and not feel flooded with volume. The goal is to deliver a message that resonates. When you write, create value for your market and client. The algorithm should help you, not control the game; it's a tool working for you. The methods and techniques will change, and you definitely want to be aware of those trends and changes. Create **messaging** that **resonates**, not stuffing the right keywords. Be aware of the tools and ratings, but avoid going so far that you put off your market or miss the mark.

"The human connection is one of the most important parts of valuable relationships and business foundations, especially in an automated world."

There is a popular saying that "AI may not replace your job, but your job will likely be replaced by someone using AI." I think this makes a lot of sense. AI is advancing at a breakneck pace, shifting from tools that streamline and support work to engines that drive growth and disrupt entire functions and industries. While early applications focused on cost savings and efficiency, AI is already starting to drive new revenue opportunities and reshape how businesses operate.

From my perspective, the role of humans has never been more critical. Yes, AI can ingest millions of records and even create a report on customer sentiment. But your customers still want to hear from *you*. They want to hear from a human. They can learn some of the business basics from a chatbot, but there are parts that they can only get from you. They want to know that you're there for them and why they should invest, especially in B2B, with you and your team. A lot of times, it is very much based on the quality of what your company specifically provides.

Human Connection

Let's use AI to help so we can be more strategic, be more human. For example, one area I recommend using AI to aid is in the "plumbing." The plumbing is the monotonous, tedious connecting of the platforms and otherwise manually moving data from one place to another. It's the extra stuff that everyone does but isn't part of your core role. These are the things you "have to do" to patch information together to get the job done.

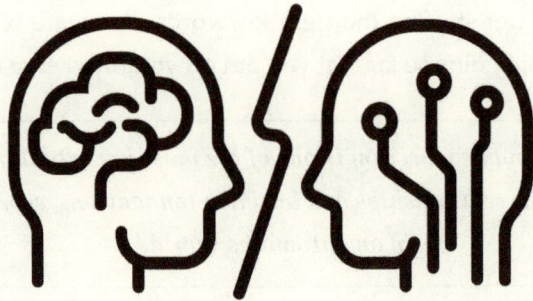

The more we can use automation and AI to draw out the results and intelligence, the more we can focus on our specific roles and how we can serve customers, build more innovative solutions, and simply make the world a better place. Think about how you can repurpose your saved time to be with your customers, be with your family, and live your life.

Customers want to know you'll be there for them. Your role is to solve their initial problems and proactively address any issues that come up. That's the purpose of their vetting: to ensure your company is the right partner and will show up for them throughout the journey.

An important part of this foundation for the human side of business is constant learning, "upskilling," and skills integration. Those who are not moving forward, who are standing still, are getting left behind now more than ever. And this doesn't mean working around the clock and getting burnt out; that's destructive. It's actually the opposite. It's an opportunity for leaders to be smart, strategic, and aware. In fact, leaders who use the latest tools, improve the processes, and partner for expertise will spend less time and have much better results and success.

Continuous Learning and Upskilling

One of the most important ways for humans to grow and move ahead is through upskilling and learning. But what are some ways to continuously learn? Too often, the term "learning" is associated only with structured courses or formal programs, but classes are just one way to learn. Learning through experience, such as taking on a new project or shadowing an expert, can be just as powerful.

You can also apply lessons from books, including this business book and many others, which offer practical, up-to-date insights grounded in proven experience. The reality is that there is no shortage of new materials, fresh ideas, applications, and videos. I'm an avid reader and lifelong learner. Clearly, you have an interest as well, since you're here.

Podcasts, TED talks, webinars, and interesting conversations are all great ways to interact with the latest information, exchange new ideas, and share thoughts. Find interactive forums or at least reflect on content after you review it to truly incorporate and apply it to your life or business. New hobbies or interests can build different creative muscles. It's also important to stay healthy and keep a clear mind. Mindset is one of the most important success factors in business.

There are, of course, formal courses for development and training, and that's going to be important. But now, there are so many other ways of learning. Things are moving so fast that, sometimes, simply absorbing articles or testing out a new AI platform will help you move a lot faster.

What do I do to stay current? I like to both absorb and share information. I am part of several different network groups and think tanks, which are also important for networking. I also like to produce and share content, such as insights on GTM practices, marketing strategy, and case studies with results on what has actually worked. I have been interviewed on podcasts and written articles because I enjoy sharing ideas and, equally, learning from others. Then, I pair this with pure learning on the latest in AI or a specific industry for one of my clients. The exchange of information and discussion with others always helps us each stay current. I mentor in courses at universities, which help the students learn, but I learn just as much from them. I love that exchange of information.

Continuous learning & refresh

Mindset, communication, leadership

Industry trends, changes

Financial models

Technology, AI

New approach to problem solving

Staying Informed

Stay informed on your industry and current events to track changes and new problems/challenges that your customer is facing. You and your company may have the solution by understanding the nuances of the industry, such as specific workflows. What information can you apply to new or adjacent industries? What's happening with specific companies or economic changes in the market? There are different angles to research and track; staying current is probably one of the best investments you can make with your time and energy. Contributing your ideas to the industry gives you a voice and reputation as a subject matter expert or thought leader.

Remember to digest and reflect on what you are learning and consuming, to better incorporate into your own strategy, the bigger purpose. This shouldn't be only a year-end, month-end, quarter-end, or after a major event. Instead, create simple strategic reflection points or sessions with your customers or teams to talk about changing market dynamics and business needs. You can step away with your team for a strategic offsite, or hit pause to reflect and look at the business from a broader perspective. Ask prompting and focused questions to understand the true impact your company is making in the market.

The goal is to think about where your business is in the market and if your actions are bringing the results you expect. Is your business on track? Are you serving the right customer base? If not, then also explore if your current marketing channels and GTM motions are leading you to the right customers for your business and offerings. Is there something you need to change, a new approach, or something new you want to bring in, something you need to let go of? For example, if your team is spread thin across multiple channels, from events to social media to high-value content, PR, etc., you can start by evaluating which is your prime GTM motion and build from there. Not all GTM motions will have equal weighting and yield equal results. Don't limit yourself to certain times of the year, a new quarter, or a new year to start something. I appreciate the concept by motivational author James Clear in his book *Atomic Habits*: "In order to improve for good, you need to solve problems at the systems level. Fix the inputs, and the outputs will fix themselves."[16]

---

[16] James Clear, "Atomic Habits Quotes," *James Clear*, accessed March 2025, https://jamesclear.com/quote/atomic-habits.

Another idea that I really like and practice is from author and inspirational speaker Simon Sinek: "Finding your why." It sounds like a simple concept, but it gives you a very big picture. What makes you tick? What's that bigger motivation for your work?

Aside from your career or job, what else do you enjoy doing? Really peel back the onion layers to figure out your "why." You can explore this for yourself, your company, and your team.

When I set up my company, I had the vision to create opportunities for people and businesses in the "rising tide lifts all boats" concept. Through marketing and GTM, we can create an abundance of opportunities for businesses and individuals, empowering them to take control of their destiny and achieve greater autonomy, providing for their families. The time has never been better to connect, collaborate, do business with others, network, share ideas, and support each other. It has never been a better time to be an entrepreneur. My "why" is a major reason why I set up the business.

Building a new business is not the answer for everyone, but the point is to find out where you can contribute and have the greatest impact. Some professionals will create a new role and a new experience within a company. Others may move to a different location to be closer to an office or family. That's been a major shift for many people. Whether you are working for a company or building your own business, you can shape your approach from how you position yourself, to understanding your ideal customer, to how you engage and build trust. The goal is to figure out what works for you and what you want to do, then align that framework with the right skills, contacts, and value you offer.

Let's look at hard and soft skills, which are timeless. I hear the term "soft skills" a lot and think of empathy, leadership, and communication. These important skills are the more subtle but often most important in terms of style, buy-in, and approach to truly move teams and shape business. Many people are so involved in the day-to-day that they haven't had a chance to just "be" or "think." Critical thinking and any form of light questioning sometimes get replaced by strict process adherence. We didn't need robots to act robotic. A great way to break this is simply to take stock periodically, have conversations, offer new innovative ideas, and better ways to get to the same result. Reach out to others, with no agenda, simply to communicate and understand what's going on in other parts of the industry; also, offer value from your perspective.

Then there are hard skills. Sometimes the soft skills are the "hard skills" because they involve human interaction, thought, and relationships. But hard skills are extremely important, the actual trade, function, and knowledge of a given field. Being able to talk in numbers and look at the financials and technology matters. Executives speak in numbers; boards of directors speak in numbers. They are investors and need to see a return on their investment. Whether in expanded business, new revenue, or greater customer affinity, it needs to be measured in some way.

There are different tools to look at. Do you want to build out new skills and be more strategic? Maybe you need to be more tactical and get involved a little bit more in the business. Maybe it's new relationships. Look at where you can partner for expertise, such as financial planning, technical configuration, or marketing strategy. These partnerships and alliances will enable you and your teams to stay focused on the core business and expertise and not be diverted. Typically, you can increase the quality and speed through these partnerships for greater medium and long-term savings.

Companies work hard to align each role to their measures of revenue, market share, profit, and customer satisfaction. A thriving business leader knows how to connect the measures and provides teams with the bigger purpose for why their work matters, too, beyond the numbers. Customers also buy for a bigger purpose beyond the numbers.

Know Your Strengths

Now ask yourself, *In what ways am I helping the company invest in what truly drives growth? How am I helping bring in more revenue? How am I helping save costs?* It's important to assess both strengths and blind spots. StrengthsFinder, now Clifton Strengths, is an effective tool because it builds on what you are good at and brings clarity.[17] The concept is to **recognize talent,** instead of focusing on weaknesses.

The concept makes sense intuitively. The traditional model aims to fix all the gaps, all the things that are wrong. Companies provide an assessment and find out their weaknesses. Then you get a long list of things to go "fix," as if they are broken. And yes, there are some derailing aspects to this. Think about sports. A coach wouldn't instruct a great kicker to bulk up and play on the defensive line. Instead, the coach would double down to help the player become even more elite in the area of talent. I use that analogy because it shows how counterintuitive it actually is to try to be great at everything. Of course, there is always the opportunity to expand into new skills, but to master core skills, keep the focus.

Look at what you are good at. What do you enjoy doing? Where can you add the most value to a problem that needs solving or use a skill that's in demand, where you can apply your talents? That's where you're going to shine, help people on your team shine, or add the most value for your clients.

We can apply the same concept to your organization. Are you and your company being seen? Is your company playing to its strengths? These practices are not only for individuals. Where is your company strong, and what is your corporate reputation? If you are looking to build a skill or share a skill, you can also look to help your community. One example would be pro bono work for an organization to showcase your talents and build your

---

[17] Gallup. "Learn About the Science of CliftonStrengths." Gallup, https://www.gallup.com/cliftonstrengths/en/253790/science-of-cliftonstrengths.aspx.

network for a win-win. Another approach is to teach at a university, where you can impact young minds and provide mentorship.

Humans and Automation

The role of humans is even more critical in an AI and automated world. We are already eliminating many of the mundane tasks such as re-entering the same information into multiple systems. Behind these transformational changes, the human thought process is setting up the systems and moving us to the next level in partnership with AI and automation.

The jobs and roles will change, and we should anticipate further change. We can also anticipate the customers' problems and pain points to provide the right solutions before we get to that point, before the customer even asks for solutions.

That's an amazing role for humans. By taking care of yourself, anticipating the different trends that are happening, understanding the industry, continuously learning, keeping yourself healthy, using some self-reflection, understanding your "why," being crisp on your hard and soft skills, and knowing what your strengths are, you can make yourself a stronger human and provide even greater impact to your business.

Tip   *Important tip: List a few of the current strengths that make you an amazing and unique business leader.*

Essentially, it comes down to identifying your superpower. In a couple of words, what would your superpower be that you can do with excellence? If you don't know or haven't thought about it, that's okay. In that case, consider it to uncover some possibilities. Start with what you are known for and what others say about you. It's only a starting point; you want to own it and feel it.

This is a great exercise for you to really think about your strengths and your company's strengths and whether there are any gaps in your perception compared to how others see you.

Connecting Humans With Automation

AI and automation continue to transform entire industries and functions, including marketing and GTM motions, completely changing how businesses operate and engage with customers. For example, marketing teams are quickly adopting AI-driven tools to personalize content at scale, optimize campaign performance, fine-tune contact lists, and review detailed analytics across channels. These advancements improve efficiency and empower marketers to make faster, data-informed decisions that drive measurable results.

I think it's safe to say we have all received an email that wasn't intended for us, maybe had the wrong name, or was outside of our industry. We silently ask, *Why am I receiving this?* The misdirected email demonstrates the risks and realities of automation without a check/balance or human oversight before wider distribution.

Sometimes, users deploy AI or automation straight out of the box, but they lack a process to verify and test. A simple test can help reconcile these issues, such as potential customers receiving a wrong email that doesn't really apply to them. Too often, the creator will blame the bots. But the true culprit is an unchecked process, leaving too much to automation, starting with a human. In reality, automation simplifies and speeds up what is already there.

Of course, automation "gone wrong" creates problems with analytics and stats, because the information is nearly irrelevant. The incorrect campaigns cause greater issues with "first impressions" and reputation over "missing stats." Be sure to test and retest with automation, especially given so many tools and communications.

I help companies with their strategy and GTM process by mapping human oversight into the process. We define automation at the right points and at the right time in the process. Successful teams take the common approach to implement one step, check it, then test it, and adjust course. CRM tools have detailed workflows, timers, and visualizations to make this easier than ever. We can create checks and balances to ensure that what we're intending goes out correctly. We're not letting the technology loose. The design and workflow will help speed up a solid process.

When we come to the technology and process chapter, we'll dive deeper into the role of humans to set up the parameters. On the human side, **we need people in place at different steps to validate and ensure that actions are correct before we move on and scale even further.**

One of the reasons people get so annoyed with spam is the sheer volume and the lack of attention to getting it right. Take the time to use personalization and avoid an aggressive, salesy tone. Fortunately, this is an area that can be adjusted and optimized, and is within our control. You can deliver a powerful message to the right person at the right time and optimize success through testing and an automated process.

"But even the best automation won't help if the core positioning and messaging don't resonate. That's where human insight makes the difference."

CHAPTER 6

MEASURING FOR OUTCOMES

Metric Mindset

Let's explore one of the most important aspects of marketing: measuring to achieve both results and larger outcomes. It's an exciting stage, because now you have your go-to-market motions in place, and you're connecting with your market. You've got this new product or service, or maybe it's your brand that you're talking about. You and your company have everything in motion, but now you want to see what's actually working. The best practice requires measuring at each step in the funnel, not waiting for a magic moment or the end of a campaign.

Today, with the right data and tools, we can see leading indicators of what's working and what may need adjustment. There is a subtle difference between measured "results" and more customer-facing "outcomes." Typically, results reflect achievements from specific actions that were taken short term. By contrast, outcomes usually reflect the impact those efforts had on the business or can do for your customer. I recommend tracking both but prioritizing outcomes to ensure your work aligns with strategic goals such as revenue growth or customer retention. For example, you might generate 150 new leads from an industry event as a result. We can measure the outcome by the number that have converted to actual customers. I often use the outcomes measures to help clients articulate their value in the market with specifics such as: "We can save you 40% in time and costs to drive efficiency."

Business results are absolutely vital, literally the scoreboard from your investments to measure market performance. Don't leave the analytics and measures to SalesOps, GTM Operations, or believe, "That's up to someone else." You might hear a less experienced marketer say, "That's finance," or "That's sales," on the numbers. But actually, it is marketing to know the marketing numbers, the company numbers. The numbers tell the story and are essentially the dashboard of the marketing machine. It is more important than ever for you to be on top of the company metrics and articulate how marketing efforts drive business. What are the leading indicator metrics telling us? In this chapter, I will unpack some of these concepts, including frameworks and takeaway summaries.

I will also provide a few definitions and the "why" behind each metric. Today, there are more potential ways to measure, more metrics than ever. Sometimes companies have so many metrics that teams get lost in the dashboard and are chasing data versus spending time to analyze the most critical ones, what the data means, and drawing insights. There is a popular saying to "measure what matters," but that also requires knowledge of the end game and insights on how to most effectively set up your dashboard. My goal here is to provide a view of the most important ones, the options, and help set you and your company up for success. You may already be doing some of this and not even realizing it.

I always recommend assessing how your GTM and marketing investments connect and contribute to revenue growth and support the larger commercial engine. What are your business results? Of course, we want to measure revenue, but that is usually a longer cycle. The same is true for measuring other **critical indicators,** such as customer satisfaction and profitability. In the meantime, measuring early indicators such as engagement and intent will help you know whether your efforts are being noticed. The problem with too much focus on early and minor customer actions is that it creates "vanity metrics" or overinflated value placed on top-of-funnel actions such as "likes" or "opened email." Instead, successful marketing teams view these early indicators as just that, indicators. Winning teams then measure conversion, or the percentage that went to the next stage. Conversion is an important measure to show the rate and volume moving through the funnel.

Let's look a little deeper at the measurements that feed into some of these foundational metrics so we can get indicators in real time. I have a lot of experience with this with complex tech tools; I want to help distill it down so you can identify the measures that best align with your goals.

From what I have seen, two extremes often happen:

1. Companies are not measuring enough and keep the **measures at too high of a level**, such as revenue. It takes too long to make adjustments, and teams can't align their goals to those needs. The intention is right in that all team members have the same metrics, but the implementation is off.

2. On the opposite end of the spectrum, some companies have **too many metrics**, and their teams are swirling in a pool of data, but missing the insights, all in the name of being "data-driven." Too much noisy data can overwhelm and hide the specific metrics you are seeking.

Instead, identify the core KPIs (key performance indicators), such as revenue, profit, customer satisfaction, number of opportunities, and time to convert, or which ones you see as most critical for your business. Then, work back to look at the metrics or indicators along the way that inform or feed into the larger KPIs, such as conversion and intent. Deal velocity or consistent speed is another metric to consider. Prospects who stay committed to the process may be further along in the funnel and closer to a decision.

Marketing Return on Investment (ROI)

Another aspect I appreciate about marketing metrics is that they help dispel an outdated stereotype that marketing is only about creatives, as if marketing equates only to working on mega-brand campaigns such as ads for the Super Bowl. Investments in marketing and sales are very visible and can make or break a business.

Successful GTM teams leverage metrics as much as or more than any other part of the business to determine what's working and what's not resonating. Data-driven measures help inform where to adjust the course and plans. We invest a lot in marketing and sales to tell the company's story and communicate our solutions. It's absolutely essential, business-critical, to know how these investments are performing. If this were a stock market portfolio, you would want to measure the performance of each investment!

Remember that we don't want to wait until all of our actions and strategies are implemented and complete. Instead, we want to be measuring all along to evaluate if the strategies are working. We talked about A/B testing. That's one very specific example, but it's a good one for measuring throughout the buyer's journey.

> *Tip: Create a one-page dashboard to show your most important metrics.*
>
> **Tip**

I always recommend creating this one-page dashboard that the whole team can work from and update. There are so many powerful tools to bring this together through automation. Of course, you will have many other pages. I've actually seen companies where it goes so deep that they have 50 or 60 pages of metrics. That's okay because it means you have solid backup details and the story behind it. But what's most important is the one page that everyone is circling around. In summary, I recommend starting with total business results, then drilling down into the details to show and evaluate what drives them.

Create your own custom dashboard with the analytics and measures that matter to your company.

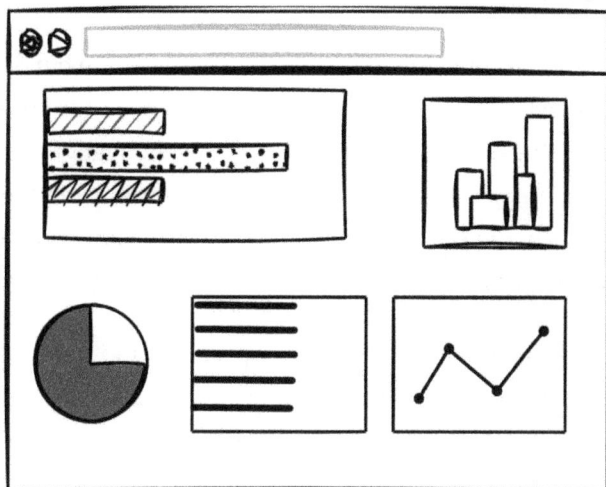

The Customer Experience

What does the company measure? Revenue? Profit? Market share? Are you gaining customers? Are you losing them? You also need leading indicators, such as the health of the pipeline, new leads, conversion, and customer satisfaction/customer loyalty. Understanding customer satisfaction requires more than a single metric. It takes ongoing feedback, behavioral insights, and outcome-based measures that tie directly to loyalty, retention, and revenue growth. Think about several levels of both leading indicators and ultimately business results.

Some companies look at how likely a customer is to recommend the solution to others, Net Promoter Score (NPS). For example, in software or SaaS of any kind, or even subscriptions, companies want to anticipate renewals or address any issues, and NPS is one measure that can help inform. With a subscription model, and it doesn't have to be SaaS, you're counting on somebody renewing every month, year, or some other time period, so in their mind, each time, they're asking, "Is this worth it?" To drive long-term success, focus on staying top of mind, delivering great service and products, and becoming the brand they trust and continue to choose.

Many times, renewals are lost not because of dissatisfaction but due to a "lack of use." The adoption didn't go well, or the customers were overwhelmed. This happens all the time in software. The customer bought into the concept, but maybe the implementation or daily usage was time-consuming or diverted too much attention to understand. With AI and more automation, customers need expertise more than ever to navigate for time-saving solutions.

Another area to watch is interface to other products and services; customers do not buy in isolation from their current tech stack. A cumbersome solution or one that lacks interface adds a time and cost investment. If your customer doesn't fully understand how to use the product, they may resort to workarounds, such as going back to a spreadsheet that "worked before" before the new solution came along. This is why customer success teams have become so important. They act as advocates who are invested in increasing adoption and satisfaction with the current solution. Someone is there with your customer, and they're not just hoping for the best. This greatly increases the opportunity for a renewal.

The metrics you collect and analyze can also help you identify patterns that point to **cross-selling opportunities**. That can mean offering additional products or services to your existing customers, such as different departments, based on their needs. The data should provide specific insights for opportunities to **upsell**, such as upgrading customers to a higher tier or selling additional products/services, which can increase both value for them and additional revenue for your business.

For example, the customer may be at a base-level tier. You show them what's possible at the next level as their business grows or requires additional capabilities. A strong marketing program gives customers exposure to what's possible but also helps them with the right category or level for their business, the right fit. The most credible and successful companies don't oversell; instead, they approach the long term through customer satisfaction and loyalty.

Ultimately we want to find the best fit for our customer. If you sell them something they don't need or won't grow into, it catches up because it's not the right solution. The company will likely not renew or reorder, and will start looking for a more cost-effective alternative or one that is a "lighter lift" on resources, whatever qualifies as a better fit for their needs.

Maybe your product or solution isn't intended to be one that they'll have forever. Instead, it solves a specific problem today. To adjust for these varying needs, you can offer tiering in your portfolio to provide different levels of products and services. Many companies offer an entry-level product/service to get started and solve an immediate problem during a business growth phase. Other times, companies price offers by size, such as the number of users or consumption of transactions. Think about where your ideal customer profile aligns with your portfolio today, but also based on a timescale into the future. Where could the business be in twelve months? Three years? Five years? **More importantly, how can your solution help your customer reach their goals?** Measure what matters.

 *Scenario*

I worked with a client reassessing how to tier and position their offerings to serve growth-stage companies better. Their original ideal customer profile focused on businesses still in the very early stages, ambitious but not yet in a financial position to invest in full-scale business advisory services. The challenge? If the company offered deep strategic support at a steep discount, it would undervalue the program and set the wrong precedent. We explored a more scalable approach to align with the end client's needs while still maintaining the brand and fostering future high-growth clients.

We created an entry-level package that was self-service with access to templates, tools, and resources. In addition, we created a community group where participants could meet together in a cohort. This is also an excellent example of using the Community GTM activation covered in Chapter 4. The program created an entry point for clients without sacrificing valuable time and resources.

I also include this approach in my portfolio and help clients bring it to market for their customers. Sometimes, the base package is the right solution to sell. I want clients to be comfortable and have a package that provides value at the right investment level for them.

By understanding the business model and metrics, I was able to create this new offering. Not every business wants to implement a fully digital platform from day one with every marketing channel. They may want to start with one channel or GTM motion. For example, they may want to double down on events or high-value thought leadership content such as articles or podcasts. They may be coming to you for "one thing."

Think of your own business: what's that one need/challenge that people come to you to solve? Maybe there are three or four different things, but it's a starting point. You can work with your client on a more comprehensive plan later, but first, you need to listen to that initial pain point and solve that problem.

Tracking the Right Data

We're now accustomed to a data-driven world, relying on metrics across nearly every aspect of business and life. While we aim to measure what matters, which metrics truly indicate progress is not always clear. I always keep in mind: *not all data points are equal.*

For example, in the last section, we touched on early indicators like **web page views,** useful as directional signals but not the ultimate measure of success.

Metrics like **click-through rates** or **demo requests** offer stronger insight as they reflect interest *and* intent.

When launching a new website, it's common to track page views initially. But the more important question is: **are those visitors taking action?** Are they downloading information, requesting a demo, or scheduling a call?

As marketers, we aim to spark interest that leads to meaningful engagement. That could mean reading an article, watching a video, or ultimately starting a conversation that results in business. Your role is to create an environment that clearly shows how you solve problems and makes it easy for the right prospects to take the next step.

AI is already reshaping how we interpret these signals. With more intelligent insights and predictive capabilities, AI can help us move beyond surface-level metrics to identify which behaviors drive conversion. It's not just about having more data; it's about making better decisions.

If you lack information or data, the next most important step is to figure out how to go out and get it. Sometimes, the best answer is the most simplistic and yet powerful: ask them. Always provide a CTA (call to action) step, a form of asking. This simple action also helps you measure buyer interest or buyer intent. If you are *not* seeing early indicators, such as views, and then later downloads or engagements, then it could be time to engage with your market directly to get more specific feedback.

For example, I often recommend and help companies with a simple survey that they can send to prospects or potential customers in their ICP to determine if their message is on track. On social media, they can do quizzes, polls, and other similar activities. Engaging with their market directly and continuously can help them keep their message current and aligned with their customers' changing needs.

You can send an email to your customer base with a few questions asking for feedback. For day-to-day communications, send a relevant article that your company published; include a few links embedded in the article, expanding on ideas to help their business. The CRM will help show where they clicked, which gives you another data point on where there is interest to learn more.

Connected Data and Information: What Is It Telling Us?

The "connected data," or "single source of truth," is another key element. We're looking at data coming in, measuring how well your message is resonating and how well your sales are converting with the different leading indicators. One source of data, or a single source of truth, keeps teams aligned and informed. If finance reports revenue from one system while sales tracks it from another, leaders may make decisions based on conflicting numbers, especially if each system maintains its own version of the customer list. This puts strategy and forecasts at risk. When both systems pull from a shared, single source, the outputs stay aligned. This doesn't mean all data must reside in one system, but there should be a single "index" or authoritative reference to determine the source data. That alignment helps avoid discrepancies across platforms, such as between a CRM and an ERP system. In smaller companies, the same concept applies.

For years, companies had data and information "living" in completely separate tools held by different departments. Then teams were blamed for being siloed. In reality, it was all procurement could do to review their data, all that finance could do to generate accurate reports at quarter end, or all that marketing could do to track new interest and conversion. Think of these systems and data as endpoints. The data was coming in after completion.

Let's compare the data and look at the reporting. **Now, we've got the opportunity, the tools, and the technology processes for fully integrated dashboards and measurements with multiple stakeholders, departments, and functions.** Each function or team can truly participate in company objectives because they are quantitatively viewing their own contribution and ROI.

Insights with the Whole Picture

Whether building the complete business dashboard or asking customers for their insights, use both quantitative and qualitative measures. In market research, we are asking "why." Peel back the onion layer to avoid incorrect assumptions about a problem.

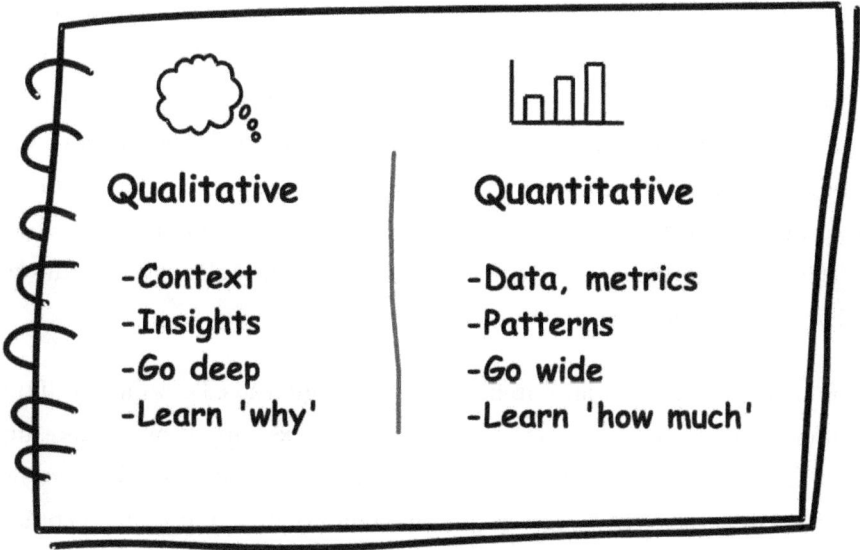

Sophisticated sentiment analysis tools and measurements are powerful and can help us get part of the picture of our market or customer base. For example, in a telecom contact center, certain tools detect when a customer is getting annoyed based on actions such as using ALL CAPS in chat, a rising voice volume, specific triggers, and keywords. On a more positive scale, there are trigger indicators when the potential customer is showing interest in learning more information or buying.

While these tools are useful and can certainly flag an upset customer or a serious buyer, they have limitations. Ultimately, the solution comes from humans developing a practical and thoughtful plan to counter a negative situation, or potentially anticipating the issues and helping to set expectations. In the same way, it will take human thought for a strategy to carefully guide an interested customer without scaring them off by being too aggressive. Create clear messages with a human touch, such as straightforward cancellation policies or payment dates, as great examples. The goal is not to trick customers. We want to create longer-term relationships and loyalty, not surprises. We start with clear messages.

Savvy marketing leaders are able to find the balance between transparency with disclaimers, but not overwhelming with long lists of issues that actually confuse buyers. Develop clear guidance and summary highlights to keep your buyers well-informed. This transparent approach enhances trust and improves the evaluation experience. You are helping them make confident, informed decisions. For example, be transparent about upcoming renewals of services. In fact, you can use the moment to highlight relevant upgrades or complementary services.

The same principle of transparency applies to digital ads. For example, if the button to close a pop-up ad is hard to find and clicks happen by mistake, the data rarely reflects true interest or intent! A better approach is to be upfront, communicate clearly, and focus on metrics that represent genuine engagement. This will help show improved metrics and also create a better buying experience.

Next, think about converting strategy into action. In reviewing the measure, what actions can your business take, and what will you do differently? For example, a marketing leader could be reviewing total acquisition cost, the complete sales and marketing spend to acquire a customer. If the costs are high in certain areas, review the ROI to determine whether the return justifies the investment or if there are ways to reduce costs while maintaining quality and impact. The goal is to keep measuring consistently without relying on a large team to pull reports manually. Despite all the tech, many companies still find it a challenge to pull clean, automated reports given different systems. But reports are improving significantly with a combination of the right processes, data sources, automation, and AI connected in the right way. Reporting will continue to improve and become more seamless over time.

The more that companies have a single source of data indexing, the cleaner the data will be and the more accurate the measures. For example, a common problem was a customer name appearing differently across CRM systems: one instance might include "Ltd," another might not, and a third could use an abbreviation. Unfortunately, the results in these cases showed the data as if these were five different companies, resulting in incomplete reporting. Clean, organized, and reconciled data at the source greatly reduces these issues.

Chasing Squirrels is Nuts

Organizing your data and processes is key to staying focused and avoiding unnecessary distractions or chasing every new trend. Another important attribute: focus. We can overschedule ourselves with too many activities and commitments, leaving us feeling run down. In the same way, we "overdo" measures and metrics. It's similar to the leaping "squirrel" again, too much distraction.

Think of it also as "add versus subtract" for a zero-sum game. If you're adding a lot of new programs but you're not adding any more resources, partnerships, technology automation, or outsourcing, you're just adding to the pile, and you're going to decrease the quality and decrease profit. But rarely do teams take the initiative to retire programs because we always tend to underestimate what it takes. Evaluating programs to pare down provides an excellent opportunity to improve quality, streamline resources, and drive up performance. These ongoing efforts and adjustments help avoid diminished returns, burned-out teams, confused customers, and poor results.

Think about your company's focus, what you do extremely well, and where you see a strong return. Consider a holistic staffing plan, especially where you are adding new workflows or initiatives. How much time will these take? Evaluate both the time needed for the initiative, but also consider the opportunity cost of what your team will not be able to cover. Often, I see companies trying to do it all versus partnering for expertise to help buy back time and resources to focus on their core business. How are you going to resource this new initiative, product, or service? Is it going to be staffing, outsourcing, or a partnership? The companies I work with always see a return on their marketing and GTM investments because they are intentional.

For example, consider where AI, together with the expertise to drive results and outcomes, could make a difference. If you are looking at the same staffing, do you need to stop or pause a different initiative or offer? Brainstorm with your team, get feedback from your partners and customers. Partnerships are crucial, especially when they bring specialized expertise that strengthens your capabilities and lets your teams stay focused. You can bring in experienced experts who've done it before and know how to accelerate results. In other cases, you may need support focused on execution, simply getting the work done, and driving progress to add bandwidth. In the end, a clear strategy keeps your team focused, so your company is pursuing goals, *not* "squirrels."

Artificial Intelligence (AI) in Data Planning

AI is moving at lightning speed and will continue to completely change the way we work. Are you including AI in your planning? Many companies count savings based on eliminating full positions, but the data shows that tasks removed by automation or streamlining don't always equate to an entire role. Some companies are seeing 20-50% productivity improvement in reduction of manual processes in contact centers, and 15-20% productivity gains for procurement professionals.[18]

There are a few different areas where you can see cost savings and improvement that AI can help you with in terms of resource and budget planning, but is AI being taken into account? The time and cost savings are so dramatic, and most platforms have integrated elements of AI across workflows in some way. Be sure to look at the efficiency gains across the company, not only by individual role or function.

Sometimes, the savings from automation, AI, and technology overall can be overestimated in the short term. For example, a department leader may be looking at AI and automation for complete headcount savings. But what if that 30% savings is across five different roles that have different skill sets? You may need to reconcile the total savings and possibly supplement with contractors, part-time headcount, or fractional resources to bridge the gap and achieve more balance. There are many practical ways to handle this successfully.

One effective strategy is to leverage fractional talent, engaging experienced, proven professionals on a part-time or project basis to gain high-level expertise without the need for a full-time role. I specialize in providing marketing and GTM strategy and execution, often serving as a fractional Chief Marketing Officer (CMO) or Marketing Strategist for companies focused on driving profitable growth. It doesn't always have to be all or nothing when you're bringing someone in to work, think part-time or on a contract. These are different ways to interpret the data and identify what actions you might take based on the insights from the metrics you defined.

---

[18] Bain & Company, "Zero-Based Redesign: The Key to Realizing Gen AI's Cost-Savings Potential," *Bain & Company*, accessed March 2025, https://www.bain.com/insights/zero-based-redesign-the-key-to-realizing-gen-ai-cost-savings-potential/.

Profitable Growth

One of the most important and often missed points is to consider growing profitably, not only driving revenue. It's very important to look at the target profitability level, especially as a business owner who is trying to move up and scale, and hire people to offload some of the responsibility for every immediate task. These efforts enable the owner or founder to focus on more strategic work and truly scale the business. For example, if you're growing your revenue but your costs are growing at the same rate, not improving your profit at the same level, you're just becoming further exhausted by spreading yourself very thin.

To overcome this, I use the Profit System™ in my advisory support to guide decisions and drive results. The system was designed by the Business Coach Academy and focuses on helping businesses reach profitable levels of growth through the right people, processes, and systems to scale. For example, one of the tools that I use in the Profit System™ helps executives and business owners move up different levels to work more "on the business" instead of "in the business" by creating the right systems, frameworks, and team structures across each function for maximum impact and true scale. This frees up executives and owners to focus on more strategic work and empowers teams, creating better opportunities for all.

Profitable growth does not mean buying market share. For many companies, profitability, primarily to reinvest in the business, has always been a core part of their mission. However, a strong focus on top-line growth became a common approach for many fast-growing companies, especially in the tech sector.

For many businesses, giving so much away upfront for pure revenue growth can be a business derailer. The "freemium" model can certainly work. But, run the numbers and have a realistic, transparent view of what it will take to balance a low-tier or free offering. Thinking through this more holistically, **there are a few ways to grow profitability.**

First is **mindset**: have a healthy, positive perspective about your business prospects. Profit creates more opportunities; it makes for a thriving business and creates momentum.

Another core element of profitability is **cost management**, keeping costs in line with growth expectations. As the company grows, what other costs do you need to consider from a foundational perspective? Think about **innovation, new ways of approaching your market,** adjacencies, and other investments to support your growth in a measured way.

Successful firms review and consider their **pricing** year on year, whether to maintain, increase, or bundle differently. This doesn't mean they are competing on price; rather, they are evaluating any market changes and economic factors and are aware of the value of competitive offers. For example, if costs are rising due to inflation or supply chain pressures on products, but pricing remains unchanged, it may signal a missed opportunity to protect margins and maintain profitability.

Or, depending on your market, maybe the **pricing structure** within the market is changing. For example, the standard may be shifting to bundling with other products or services. In B2B, many companies are adopting consumption-based pricing models, or "usage-based" instead of time or number of seats in software. One company with a data platform charges based on compute usage, while cybersecurity providers may price according to the number of endpoints monitored, aligning cost with actual value delivered.

In this case, consider your own **business modeling and scenario planning** to reduce pricing in one area, but increase services or some of the add-ons in another area. A company could upsell complementary products and services or provide a new layer of tiering, given the market shifts and changing needs. Review pricing levels, considering new customers too. Based on learnings from your experience, model if additional new services could be offered to improve their experience, such as customer support or customized services.

Top companies in their category look for ways to **move up the value chain** and offer a greater level of service, with higher impact. Over the years, I have helped companies define their core offering, introduce tiering, and add-on or optional services. Companies are typically motivated to reduce costs and save time! They accomplish these goals by **automating more routine tasks** to free up more time for strategic work so executives can spend time with customers, create new solutions and revenue streams, or focus on innovation to positively impact the world.

Hidden Costs

I often hear from business leaders who ask, "Do we need to change our workflow and processes?" Reviewing your workflow and processes is at the heart of eliminating inefficient operations and unnecessary costs. On the positive side, the process may be running smoothly, team members follow it, and although manual, it works. Of course, there are short-term switching costs associated with any change. But in the medium and long term, an updated process infusing automation, AI, and the right expertise can bring significant savings.

If you choose the right tool or technology, you'll often see cost savings. But it's important to factor in the **investment** required for training and transition. We'll cover more in detail in the next chapter, both technology and process. You can reduce the risk of a new system by running it in parallel with the legacy one during rollout, using the old system as a backup. Plus, sticking with inefficient processes will definitely cost more over time, and your company can run the risk of falling behind faster, more innovative competitors.

As we covered in the last chapter, incorporate skill-building and **invest in your team as you update processes and incorporate best practices and automation.** Review where team members can take on more strategic work, add more value, and grow. They can often learn more from working on a new project to stretch their capabilities. The assignment doesn't have to be a new position or role; it could be a new project. Whether it's one team member mentoring another, cross-functional teams collaborating, or partnerships between companies, the principle remains the same.

Take the opportunity to consider where to let go of less profitable business as you grow, or partnerships that are less synergistic. Maybe the customer or partner now falls outside of your target profile or isn't the best fit given changing market needs. As part of your strategy, you can review which customers make sense to work with directly and which are ideal to work through a partner. Consider developing an alternative track focused on a DIY, self-service, or community-driven model. The goal is to remain aware of profitability from multiple angles, including time, team capacity, workflows, and operational processes.

Aligning Metrics

Rightfully, there is a lot of focus on driving revenue. As marketing professionals, we look at how we can help the company overall. As an executive, I always focus on how my team can support company KPIs and how the company scorecard translates to the department, aligning strategy and day-to-day execution.

Your marketing measures are part of the larger company scoreboard. How do marketing, sales, and customer success contribute to the overall revenue, profit, customer satisfaction, long-term growth, and innovation? Understanding the answer to that question and influencing the direction is critical. To drive real business impact, marketing, sales, and other GTM functions need to align their goals with the company's key metrics, such as revenue, profit, market share, EBITDA, or customer satisfaction. However, we still need leading indicators along the way to measure the effectiveness of specific programs and initiatives. Otherwise, the measures will be too distant from specific operations. A healthy balance with the company goals tied to department measures can solve this dilemma.

For example, the company needs to evaluate whether a specific event, which typically involves major investments in sponsorship, travel, and opportunity cost, delivered the anticipated or desired results. There is an element of marketing and sales to weigh in, but it's a company investment. In the same way, don't wait for sales data to find out what potential or current customers think about your new product. Test along the way, continue to research, and talk to your market. However, the ultimate measures, such as sales revenue, will hit the P&L. Measuring smaller activities along the way will give you a solid leading indicator.

Marketing is an investment that helps generate revenue or, put more simply, **marketing is a revenue generator**. It's an investment, because you will get a greater return than what was put in. It's truly a "miss" when marketing is labeled as a cost center. There is, of course, the opportunity to position the capabilities correctly or evaluate if you are fully articulating the return on investment. I love this quote by global management consulting firm McKinsey & Company:

> *"When marketing is at its best, it's actually a growth driver. Chief Marketing Officers (CMOs) who realize that do two things: First, they take a growth mindset and set bolder aspirations for marketing. Second, they recast marketing as a revenue driver versus a cost center."*[19]

This is certainly a conversation that's going on within most industries and the marketing function. Marketing is not alone; I see this same analysis for most functions: what is working well, and what is the potential to impact the business? In the case of marketing, the opportunity is to communicate a well-positioned message, lay the groundwork to set up for sales, and drive revenue. To accomplish this successfully, companies invest in their brand,

---

[19] McKinsey & Company, "Quote of the Day: October 9, 2023," *McKinsey & Company*, accessed March 2025, https://www.mckinsey.com/featured-insights/quote-of-the-day/october-9-2023.

reputation, and story to share with the market in many different forms. Then, they tell that story in different channels with different formats of content. We measure it and adjust course based on the insights we've gained and the results achieved. On a deeper level, we truly connect with our market.

Tip: What are the three metrics that are most
Tip *critical to your overall business?*

What are the three most critical metrics for the business that will indicate the level of progress and success? Articulate the flow-through metrics for GTM, including marketing and sales functions, which have a common set of measures that tie back to the company metrics.

CHAPTER 7

PROCESS AND TECHNOLOGY

Tech is Everywhere

It's no surprise that technology impacts every industry, role, and person at some level. Process and technology work closely together, and the two are tightly connected for several reasons:

- Automation without process automation simply means your teams will do the same things faster, but not necessarily better. Look for effectiveness in addition to efficiency to provide customer excellence and reduce unnecessary costs.

- Start by documenting and evaluating the process before optimizing, especially if you have new technology planned.

- Often, new tools and automation provide the opportunity to change the workflow or process to reflect best practices based on experience. Many companies simplify their processes when they take on a new technology.

- The "lean movement" aims to eliminate unnecessary steps and optimize processes. It first started in manufacturing but is now widely used in business operations, and is especially important for large software platform rollouts such as a new CRM, ERP, or HR system. Change management and transformation initiatives typically accompany these initiatives to take advantage of the opportunity to streamline processes.

Automation will definitely help, but I always work with clients to first optimize their steps and workflow before automating. For example, in marketing, look at the number of handoff points for review cycles, such as within the RevOps (revenue operations) process. Many teams focused on GTM are now combining marketing operations and sales operations into a RevOps team and function instead of separating marketing and sales operations. Companies can eliminate manual steps in invoicing, onboarding, or order processing through AI and automation technology, reducing costly and monotonous tasks such as scanning, reconciling, and emailing.

The technology plus process change reduces some of these frustrating tasks, such as hard-to-read signatures, varying document formats, and long cycle times from receipt to payment.

When ready for automation, here are ways to incorporate and alternatives:

- Automation covered within platforms (e.g., CRM and ERP systems); the platform provider incorporates automation, reducing the need to "stitch" together multiple smaller applications. Platforms may also incorporate advanced AI functionality such as Large Language Models (LLMs) or AI agents.

- Custom automations through technology such as RPA, low code, or workflow automation tools like Zapier will bridge applications and port data or actions, typically working with structured data (typically organized in a defined format and fields, making it easier to retrieve).

- AI can definitely be customized through model training and application to a given business. Think of AI as a layer on top, working with unstructured data. AI also does more than pure processing of the data. It can start to draw conclusions, make predictions based on patterns and learning.

- Where automation simulates actions and "doing," AI simulates "thinking" by serving up insights, information to make decisions, and the ability to personalize on a massive scale.

I often hear comments such as, "Doesn't it feel like everything's technology-driven today?" I've also heard the phrase, "We're all in tech now, living in a data-driven, always-on world." Technology is met with different views: many welcome modernization and see it as positive. Others view it with skepticism, concern for how it will be used, or the need for investment and change. As with any change, there are advantages, concerns, and risks.

As consumers, we're experiencing this tech shift, too. We're seeing a lot more technology enter our lives, certainly in the workforce and in the buying process. We live it every day, from ridesharing to online groceries to social media updates or reviews.

Ironically, the same is true for technologists adapting to customer needs. IT teams and engineers are investing more time and energy in truly understanding business, researching the market, and identifying customer pain points and needs.

I can draw a parallel here to financial literacy. Just as it's essential to know the numbers and be financially and commercially savvy, today, we have to be tech-savvy to a basic level to stay ahead or fall behind. A marketing leader isn't in finance, but does need to know their numbers to be effective. If you think of tech in the same way, it makes sense. Encourage teams to embrace technology and understand the potential from a business perspective and the outcomes it can drive.

It's not just your perception; technology has absolutely changed, even disrupted, businesses. We can all think of businesses that have been revolutionized by a combination of tech and process: from Blockbuster to Netflix, taxi services to Uber, and even how we order books or birthday presents and have things delivered with Amazon. In B2B, SaaS completely changed the business model to a subscription and service model, providing applications with enterprise efficiency. Think of all the different technologies that you have your hands on today that weren't even around five years or even ten years ago, such as GenAI for the masses (ChatGPT, Claude, etc.) or AI agents.

Having a certain level of tech understanding is healthy and can be thought of in the same way as having a pulse on the financials and the changes, measuring the ROI, and looking for impact. Let's take a look at some of the drivers of technology. We can review the historical evolution to understand the pattern, and it may help you put it into context as well as understand where we're going from here. To look ahead to the future, it's important to look at it in the context of the past and present.

Tech-Driven Business Transformation: How We Got Here

Over the last two decades, tech-driven business transformation has reshaped how organizations operate, compete, and deliver value. It has evolved from digital transformation and cloud migration to advanced analytics and now to generative AI and agentic AI.

Global technology and consulting firm IBM notes, "Digital transformation is a business strategy initiative that incorporates digital technology across all areas of an organization. It evaluates and modernizes an organization's processes, products, operations and technology stack to enable continual, rapid, customer-driven innovation."[20]

---

[20] Keith O'Brien, Amanda Downie, and Mark Scapicchio, *What Is Digital Transformation*, IBM Think, https://www.ibm.com/think/topics/digital-transformation.

The information age, including digital transformation, is part of a broader paradigm called "Industry 4.0." Let's look at the different phases of the industry for context and what is meant by these phases. The terms may sound as if they apply to manufacturing, but there is a broader aspect across industries that impacts all of society in many different ways. Here is a look at the different phases that are generally recognized and understood in these definitions.

Industrial Revolution Phases

Phase	Shift	Attributes
Industry 1.0	Hand tools to automation	Steam and water power
Industry 2.0	Custom to mass production	Factories, assembly lines, electricity
Industry 3.0	Computing power	Computers and automation in manufacturing
Industry 4.0	Digitization and digitalization	Smart systems, integration of IoT, artificial intelligence, cloud computing, cyber
Industry 5.0	Humanization and personalization	Collaboration between humans and robots, AI

Industry 1.0 was the first major shift, moving from hand tools to the wide-scale use of machines with the introduction of steam and water power. Imagine the impact this had on the production supply chain, food, and energy. The shift was moving from hand tools to automation.

Industry 2.0 was essentially the shift to mass production and factories, which came about with assembly lines. During this same era, electricity was introduced. These massive societal shifts impacted every person, profession, and way of life. Suddenly, jobs moved to the cities and factories, creating new opportunities.

Industry 3.0 was the start of digital automation. Think about the first computers and significant changes to improve automation in manufacturing.

Then, **Industry 4.0** arrived. Many would say we are in this phase now and starting to transition to the next phase. Industry 4.0 brings in the shift and key attributes around digitalization and digitization, including the "Internet of Things," such as smart watches, biosensors, and meters/measures. But even more broadly, AI comes into widespread usage and application. No longer under development or in trials, it's being widely used. Yet, the technology is still in its infancy in many ways, and we are only at the start. Cybersecurity and cyber as a category have also taken hold. The point is that things are moving in mega shifts, and we're part of it. It's truly an exciting time.

Industry 5.0 is equally inspiring and revolutionary. In 5.0, we move into true human-machine collaboration and personalization. We will see hyper-personalization, which is a shift from largely standard products.

There are also different phases of the internet that underlie each of these and provide further capabilities at each stage (web 1.0, web 2.0, web 3.0, etc.).

Driving Forces and Buyer Needs

As part of this transition, mobility has evolved rapidly with the confluence of smart devices, increased power and bandwidth, and the absolute explosion of apps. As a leader in telecom, I was part of driving the shift to mobile-first experiences, bringing the power of computing, apps, and convenience into the palm of the hand. Absolutely revolutionary! Consumers and business users want information when and where they want. For communications, the path went from landlines to cell phones, voice only, to SMS with some data. It was the smartphone that came into play to put computing power in your hand and create true mobility. Everything became mobile. It's hard to imagine a time when we didn't have all of this literally at our fingertips.

Social media brought two-way conversations into play. Communications were no longer one-way, download. Now, there was a way to "crowd-source" information, insights, and chat regardless of quality. Transparency went mainstream.

Suddenly, communication of major events was playing out with individual creators. This opened up, and continues to open up, completely new ways of conducting business.

Before social media, most public information was one-way; communication was centralized. The shift in mobility and connectivity fueled the cultural side of social media, driving information to be "instant" and "in the moment." There are no scheduled times to get information. As we look at technological change, we have to look at the evolution of where our technology has evolved from, overlaid with business and consumer needs and wants. For example, we can understand at a deeper level what our customers want and the human behavior and needs driving these changes.

Several years ago, many companies invested in digital transformation, modernizing technology, streamlining processes, and shifting toward integrated application suites and connected workflows to reduce manual effort. IT started as "computer maintenance" and then moved rapidly to take on a very important role in driving the technology strategy for a company. The CIO (Chief Information Officer) and IT took front-and-center roles within companies because they became involved with the connection of data, implementing business applications, managing the complete network, and cybersecurity. The goal was to connect it all, building a robust infrastructure and the right backbone of servers. The cloud came into play, which provided more of that connectivity, and SaaS became essential. You didn't have to have everything on-site. It fed into this world of safety and backup, but you could access things everywhere.

This digital transformation completely changed the way that we work. It's almost unrecognizably different from just a few years ago.

Companies invested in marketing and sales tools to leverage technology changes. In fact, marketing always needs to stay on top of technology changes to automate the many functions, tie together data across systems, and ultimately get the right message to the right person.

Enter AI

We are moving at dramatic speeds into powerful use cases with AI. The technology takes automation to a completely unprecedented level. Marketing and GTM are harnessing these changes, given the need for personalization, customization, and driving revenue.

Of course, there is also hype about AI, but that is also driven by its incredible potential and significant time and cost savings. The medical breakthroughs, security capabilities, and communication improvements with AI are only the start.

The secret is to look at real uses, real return on the investment in time, applications, AI agents in order to solve problems. In many ways, artificial intelligence is building on what was there for automation, which preceded AI.

Large language models in AI, generative AI, are an important aspect of the technology. They're very powerful, especially in marketing, making it easy to create outlines, refine ideas, and assimilate and pull together large data sets. AI began by learning from large volumes of existing data to generate results, and it is now rapidly evolving to not only analyze but also model complex patterns and generate entirely new content.

GenAI is looking for patterns, making quick assessments, and giving instant information, graphics, and ideas. And it's moving, becoming even more predictive and accurate at modeling. A massive amount of information has already been consumed in training these models. Most companies are leaning into AI investments through proofs of concept and strategies to streamline processes, eliminate tedious work, and improve accuracy. **AI agents** take it a step further by acting autonomously on behalf of users, completing tasks based on goals, context, and real-time data.

Agentic AI workflows and orchestration coordinate multiple agents and systems to work together seamlessly, enabling end-to-end automation across complex processes.

Quantum computing is beginning to take shape with early breakthroughs showing potential for AI acceleration, complex problem-solving, and next-generation security. It's even more scientific, but it's looking at modeling and solving very specific problems ahead of the curve.

In medicine, quantum computing explores how to simulate clinical trial design so we can reduce the costs and time needed. Financial modeling leverages quantum computing. In marketing, an ad agency or a marketing team could potentially use quantum optimization to simulate millions of ad spend scenarios, selecting the most profitable one in seconds.

The long-term impact on computing and automation promises to be transformative. The point is that there's no shortage of information out there, so look at how to put it to use for what you need. But find the right application of the technology to drive business results.

Turning Data Into Information and Insights

The last two decades were focused on connecting the systems and modernizing for digital transformation. The opportunity now is: **How do we best use this data?** When data is pulled directly from a system, it's often raw data, numbers, and stats. While the data might be interesting, it's not particularly useful without context or interpretation. The next step is turning the **sea of data into** *useful* **insights** for you and your business to help efficiency, serve your customers, and manage the business.

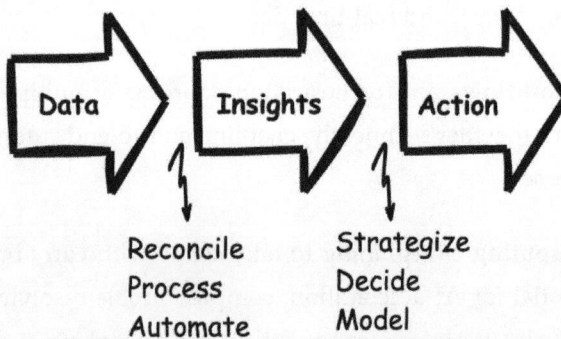

Data → Insights → Action

Reconcile Strategize
Process   Decide
Automate   Model

For example, a marketing leader reviews data in CRM. Instead of presenting the raw data, the marketing leader can start with the dashboard, but also focus on the most important elements depending on the business, new customers (new logos), new geographic locations, conversion, or even the length of the sales process. Step back and look at what the data is saying and which part of the story to focus on. What conclusions can be drawn from it? With the right configuration, you can use the technology to help serve up those insights relative to your business.

Eventually, you'll want to get into some business modeling to help show various scenarios. For example, pull out the current data and then model different scenarios such as various revenue levels, which customers will renew or stay on, or the potential impact of adding a new product or service.

I have built many of these models for companies of different sizes in different industries. Independent of the industry or market, one of the best practices I share is to keep it simple, avoid measuring the impact of too many different variables. Instead, keep it focused and isolated to a specific changing variable, such as revenue, gross margin, or new pipeline (new customers), and then use variations of the model to assess other factors. The ultimate goal is to tie potential company actions to the business model to forecast where you will see the most likely and greatest returns.

Reviewing raw data in the CRM is simply getting the data. As business leaders, we need to drive action and look at what the data is telling us and how to use that for our business. You add value as a marketer and businessperson when you interpret the data, make recommendations, and help plan the future, not react to a set of numbers. Think about automation; the goal is to connect and "make happen" actions that do not require further overview, interpretation, or oversight. By contrast, you can work with the information, draw conclusions, propose ideas, and pull together the data in a unique way to highlight new possibilities. The human-machine balance brings the best of both worlds, even with advanced AI systems.

What do your customers truly want? What are some of their unmet needs that they're not even talking about? To achieve success, you'll need to connect the dots and create a unique strategy.

I believe there's phenomenal technology available, but I think the success criteria come down to how you use it. To get started, look at the processes and technology in place today and the data you are able to retrieve. Can you draw conclusions and get business insights from this information? Too often, I see companies trying a variety of technology tools, but missing the opportunity to simplify their processes or focusing on one or two dimensions. The result is overwhelming raw data that is not helpful to the forecasting process.

However, definitely stay on top of emerging tech trends. Many leaders actively seek expert guidance on what's ahead, where to invest, and how to navigate change. Staying informed and forming a clear point of view helps you stay relevant, make better decisions, and apply innovation in ways that truly benefit your business.

How Technology and Processes Help Automate Marketing

Let's look more specifically at applying technology and the right processes to marketing. Identify *where* technology can help streamline and automate your business efforts. Automation will not only help reduce costs but also improve quality and free up your team to spend time on more value-added work.

Time to be human. The right automation of manual tasks, such as consolidating lead data from multiple event sources into a central system, will free up your team's time. Your company will have more time for higher-value work, such as building client relationships, shaping strategy, and launching new products and services. Automation drives up value, internally and for customers; it is one of the main use cases and goals. You are essentially hiring another "specialist." The automation and simplified process will help the team across different roles if done in the right way.

Think about it as *how* you are applying technology and AI. I help companies evaluate which technology is right for them by starting with their current state and looking at what they want to achieve. The transformation comes from the goals and the commitment to change, not only from the platform. The real power is in the people, process, and goals. The technology, whether AI-powered tools or new applications, helps them get where they want to go.

Meanwhile, your competitors are also evaluating new technology and processes to be more lean and solve problems for the market. Your competitive edge matters. Through the right use of technology, you can do things faster and smarter. The situation is shifting at a record pace. Companies that don't embrace technology risk falling behind or being disrupted because they can't keep up with those who are using the tools to their advantage. And it's not just technology for the sake of technology. The pace of business is so fast that incorporating technology is no longer optional. Without it, both well-established and emerging companies will struggle to compete, innovate, and keep up with changing customer expectations. With more data, channels, and faster decision cycles, technology becomes essential to stay responsive and relevant. That's the competitive side.

Ironically, AI and automation can help companies provide a **better customer experience** when done right. Start with a simple but important aspect of your business, such as where technology can help with basic FAQs (Frequently Asked Questions). Do you really want your human staff taking these basic, repetitive questions that could be answered online or by a chatbot? For example, digital solutions take the burden off your team by answering questions such as hours of operation for a local business or viewing a demo for a software-based business. Cover those business basics without having to get a human involved. Save your team for the discussions with customers, applying your products and services to solve their challenges.

I think of a pyramid or layers of information. Save the human expertise to untangle more complex elements or have more engaged conversations to build relationships. For example, imagine yourself calling in on a helpline. You simply want to get the information, not navigate through endless options. Most companies prioritize providing personal support for more complex issues. But for routine tasks such as booking appointments or answering routine questions, they leverage technology such as AI agents, which saves time on both sides and can improve the customer experience.

Operational efficiency is one of the main reasons why companies leverage technology. They also use it for repeatable processes to drive predictable responses. There's more data now to see what's working in a business and then inform the decision-making. Customers seek solutions, and you aim to capture even more precise measurements than ever before with the goal of providing those solutions. Automate manual tasks and processes to increase productivity, allowing your team to focus on higher-value work. These higher value activities could be connecting with ideal customers or delivering an exceptional customer experience for those already on board.

One of the attributes to look for as a buyer seeking technology solutions is quantifiable data. Companies now promote the percentage of time savings or efficiency you can expect. For example, "This program, on average, provides 30% time savings," or "Your team can process claims in minutes versus three business days with previous solutions." Sometimes, with AI, we're seeing process steps go from weeks to minutes or seconds. These returns are impressive, but it's important to quantify the anticipated results to truly understand the impact as well as what assumptions were made (such as the effort required, any other systems needed, etc.).

While increased productivity definitely frees up resources to enable investments in new growth areas, markets, and product services, that doesn't mean technology can help with **innovation** or brainstorming. For example, I have worked with some powerful collaborative whiteboard tools for virtual teams to use around the world. But despite these powerful resources, real innovation still requires human insight. **It's a combination of the best of both; technology enables the process, but your perspective and expertise drive the value.**

Customer expectations are another driver for continuous improvement and pace. I can't tell you how many clients I've worked with who now want to have an e-commerce site because there's a *consumer expectation* based on what they've seen with Amazon, and they have real demand from their market base. This same "easy" experience is, of course, now expected in B2B and even B2G. Of course, not every product or solution lends itself to e-commerce, but every business has an expectation and *need* for a very simplified approach and way to do business. For example, notice the popularity of the one-button click for call to action (CTA) such as "learn more," "book a demo," or "contact us." We hardly think about it anymore!

"We need to make it easy for people to do business with us, whether it is how to receive more information or, at the core, making it clear what we offer."

Not every offering will be sold through e-commerce. But imagine if you could take part of your product or service line, make it available online, and make it a little more of a DIY or self-service model. That frees up your team and makes it easy for your customers. Without updated technology and streamlined processes, your business may already be falling behind. The good news? Putting the essentials in place no longer requires a massive investment when approached consistently over time. The tools, expertise, and frameworks are all available.

Talent Paired With Technology

Earlier, I covered the critical role of the human aspects of marketing through people. Teams must not only keep up with change, they must make sense of the change and find the opportunities. **Technology will continue to evolve, but it's people who interpret, adapt, and drive meaningful results.** In fact, the more advanced the tools and tech become, the more valuable human judgment, creativity, and connection become. This reinforces the importance of people working alongside tech and with processes to add true value.

The best leaders and companies **invest in people**, not only in technology and tools. When it comes to technology, make sure that your employees can tie and stitch together the systems and bridge communication gaps. For example, you can create tremendous efficiencies and time savings by having your teams on connected messaging platforms. This might take some training and investment, but it pays off. You will definitely need to invest in soft skills to develop and refine human interactions, such as being able to sell, handle difficult conversations, express empathy, and communicate. Investing in people does not always mean sending them to a training class. Training and courses are important, but only one component. Invest time in mentoring from leaders or SMEs, assigning new projects, online programs, or teaming up cross-functional roles to learn from each other and collaborate.

This work is more important than ever, especially as many larger companies scale back formal training, relying instead on the abundance of online learning platforms like Coursera, LinkedIn Learning or even YouTube to fill the gap. While there's more content available than ever before, the responsibility now often falls on individuals to take initiative and apply their learnings.

Targeted coaching and guidance make a difference. I help teams not only identify the right skills but also apply them through hands-on learning, whether it's business modeling, creating a messaging framework, soft skills, or project-based work. It's incredibly rewarding to see team members grow in confidence and capability when they have the right support.

📖 Scenario

Tying this all together, there is a strong correlation between process, technology, and people. That impact from consumer markets continues to influence the B2B space, such as with "the click of a couple of buttons." It's human nature; we want things instantly, and that's naturally permeating into the business B2B software platforms as well. We are more aware of our limited resource of *time* than ever before.

Let me give you an example of this intersection between people, processes, technology, and usability. As part of new product development, I focused on understanding the customer's environment and pain points to help create solutions that solve real problems and would be practical to use. As part of product marketing, I was able to gain customer insight, conduct market research, and understand the perception of a product concept in the early days of building out those products. In one of the projects that I worked on with a software application, the key customers didn't really understand how to use the products in this new software interface and program. They loved the concept and the way it was designed, but it was just too open, too configurable, and not practical.

The customers couldn't wrap their heads around it. They knew they would have to spend a lot of time understanding what was possible and building it out themselves, and of course, that didn't appeal to them. Instead, we discussed what would work, what they preferred to have it templatized as a starting point, and where they wanted the freedom for custom configurability.

Our team incorporated this feedback to iterate on the design. After refreshing the application and design, we went back to a smaller subset of the customers to validate. This new version hit the mark! In fact, they went on to buy the solution. This is a best practice for software platforms, offering a few templates that reflect the different types of users and a place to get started, giving them the tools to make changes and be able to adjust and reconfigure. It's tempting to make everything "configurable," but in the end, the users want to dive in and appreciate a starting point with many applications and platforms. Part of the value they are buying is the expertise in the configuration.

That's just one example of applying a combination of user and customer feedback to make the technology more powerful. I often advise companies to simplify their tech stack, integrate platforms, and clearly map the workflow. A well-defined workflow outlines the processes and shows how work actually gets done.

Building the Right Tech Stack

In marketing, as CMOs, we often talk about the tech stack. This is literally a group of technology investments such as the CRM, content platforms, lead capture tools, website analytics, or social media connectors. Other examples in the tech stack could include contact enrichment so you have the right contact info for outreach lists, or even video or webinar platforms.

The tech stack is important, but so are the processes and people. In fact, it's even more important because you have to get the processes right. It really takes all three:

- People
- Processes
- Technology

If you have strong tech but poor processes and untrained teams, then the operation will not be efficient and error-prone. If you have good people but lack the right processes or tech, the business will also be inefficient and basically rely on heroes to do a lot of diving and catching. I think we've all seen these two scenarios.

Then, if you have strong processes and tech but not the right team members or talent development, then the business is still not leveraging investments properly. But, sometimes, teams get caught up in too much tech, back to that *squirrel*! We see it all the time, diving after the latest trend, but it is time-consuming and costly to implement new tools and subscriptions, and it has to add enough value to be worth the time and investment. Teams need to evaluate, "Does this help the business, add enough value? What are the alternatives?" Too often, leaders underestimate the onboarding and adoption needed. Top partners, especially in software, understand the implementation phase and help streamline the setup and adoption.

During planning or implementation, processes are often remapped to eliminate steps. There is a balance between sticking with your current process built around different workflows or tools, or shifting to:

1. A best practice advocated by a platform partner (based on experience).
2. A custom configuration to adapt the technology to your company's processes.

There are pros and cons to each. The pendulum has swung more recently towards "out of the box" or more standard configurations. This approach is more economical for the buyer in the short term but also enables the buyer to have more future options, such as interfacing with other platforms and programs. This is another advantage of templates and not reinventing the wheel at every step. Website creation is a great example that has come down significantly in cost and price due to the standardization of templates with plug-in elements and images to customize.

The entire function of customer success has completely taken off in the last few years, especially to drive adoption and increase renewals for subscription-based businesses. The company wants you to adopt the solution so that you renew, but they also want you to have a great experience. I often help clients evaluate their tech stack and look at the best match for what they need based on my experience and unbiased view. I can really help my clients hone in on what's needed for them and make sure they will be set up for success. Taking care of current customers is essential in any industry.

Scenario

Process changes are all relative. Sometimes it makes sense to remap a process and then automate. With the pace of AI, the workflow and processes are already changing at a dramatic rate, eliminating steps and connecting information. Many companies I work with start small, build momentum, and then scale wider. It's a smart approach. For example, when they roll out a new platform, they create a plan to improve the processes along the way to set themselves up for long-term success. These companies take the opportunity to simplify steps, automate, or even eliminate certain actions. Start with a collaborative workshop to identify the end game state, goal, and what success looks like. You can use this approach whether it's a new ERP rollout, CRM, QA system, etc.

Bring the team along as part of that change management. As you map out your workflow or process, ask yourself: *What steps could be eliminated? Could some things be combined? Could fewer people be involved in the process, so there are fewer handoffs?* I've helped many clients manage their analytics and dashboards to review their progress and process. This almost always results in the need for leveling up, helping team members grow, and learning a new tool or technology. In fact, sometimes a new role needs to be created, or an existing role should be merged with another role.

I see a pattern where companies underestimate how much time and thought it takes to create high-quality content, not mass-produced filler, but standout stories, thoughtful articles, engaging videos, and a steady drumbeat of compelling posts. It always looks effortless from the outside.

AI can help in all aspects, such as speeding up drafts, surfacing ideas, and handling repetition, but it's not a magic fix. Quality still requires judgment, creativity, and context. The most impactful content blends smart use of AI with a human touch that understands the market, the moment, and the message. Tools and platforms powered by technology, such as AI, assist in repurposing various styles and formats of content.

For example, you can easily turn the content from a comprehensive whitepaper into an article, a few social posts, an email series, or even a webinar. Pull out the key points, unpack the story, and add valuable context with consistency across all of the channels.

This is another practical example of people, processes, and technology working together in sync. I enjoy helping clients build their businesses using this approach. Now, let's take a closer look at automation.

Automate the "Plumbing"

Automation is possible at many different stages. It can underlie processes, speed up steps, connect information, and remove repetition, such as entering information from one program to another (sometimes called "swivel chair"). There is an opportunity to connect systems, connect information, and streamline "the plumbing."

Think about plumbing as connecting the pieces together through different pipes of information or data. Connect related tasks to free up time for more strategic work. For example, link opt-in customer contacts across your internal platforms, especially if your teams manually pull names or product purchases from one system and enter them into another. In that case, it's not only time-consuming but introduces errors and is a clear sign that automation could drive major efficiency.

Manual work introduces quality issues because information can be transposed or missed. There are tools out there to bridge data across different platforms, and many different software suppliers are already connecting themselves to different platforms, so this automation happens through integration. Look at where automation makes sense, and just as important, where it does not make sense. Where are you ready to automate, and where could it actually hurt your business? Long before AI, buyers complained about receiving robotic emails or direct messages on social platforms that felt impersonal, and spam was born. In the same way, when automation is used without careful training or oversight, it leaves a poor first impression.

Unfortunately, it's a common pitfall and one you'll want to avoid. A smart way to leverage automation without hurting your reputation is by mapping out your process and ensuring it runs smoothly in its current state. Only then should you layer in automation.

Automation can dramatically improve marketing efficiency, but communication can sound robotic and impersonal without personalization. Use automation to *trigger* personalized outreach based on real customer behavior. Like in chess, plan a few moves ahead. For example, a customer downloads a whitepaper on optimizing the Customer Experience (CX) in their contact center. Next, automation will trigger a series of steps called a sequence:

- **First email**: Thank the customer for downloading *the CX whitepaper* and offer a related checklist or resource, such as a customer journey mapping template.

- **Second email**: Invite them to a webinar specifically focused on the same theme but deeper, such as "modernizing CX strategies."

- **Third touch**: Based on engagement, send a personal follow-up note referencing the importance of Customer Experience and offering a short consultation to apply to their business.

This method keeps outreach timely and efficient (through automation) while ensuring the content feels relevant and human (through personalization). The result is better engagement, stronger relationships, and a far better first impression. Humans do their thing, and the bots do theirs.

That's a great example of using technology effectively. It is worth the time and effort to map the process, connect the right tech/automation, AI, and leverage the expertise of your human team. Larger companies have dedicated roles to specifically integrate technology, such as "martech" (marketing technology), "sales ops" (sales operations), or "RevOps" (revenue operations). These roles have become mission-critical across businesses over the past few years. The need still exists even if you don't have someone fully dedicated to these functions, especially in a smaller company. Someone must review the metrics, dashboards, and incoming data, and then have the technical and marketing expertise to connect systems like the CRM, automate the right processes, and generate reports. Without that, it's easy to look at incomplete or wrong data and make decisions based on it. The responsibility for the data starts with the executive team, and then having the right team in place to pull together the right information.

> ⚡ **Tip** *Helpful tip: Start by mapping how a prospect's inquiry flows through your systems.*

Whether it's a small company or a large enterprise, look at how a lead makes its way through the system. Follow the journey of a prospect in your system. Where does that information go? Who's involved? What data gets captured? Where is that stored? How does that flow through to the next person?

Then assess whether that person is interested in engaging further *now*. What is the next step? For example, is a call set up? What if it's someone who could be interested in the future? Your team can add that lead to what's called a nurture campaign, where they're going to receive updates and hear from you periodically. What if they're not interested? Do they want to unsubscribe, or do you want to check in with them in the future?

All of these elements require someone with technical expertise to properly set up and configure them within your system. Of course, your marketing team or marketing agency will drive the systems. But as a business leader, you are ultimately responsible for shaping the customer's experience and ensuring there is a clear path to your sales team, executive team, or the business owner in a smaller business.

Automation removes the need for manual tracking across multiple lists, but it's important to stay intentional. As teams add tech, CRM systems become more sophisticated, and related tools become more complex, making it easy for data management to spiral out of control. To avoid this, establish clear processes for entering, maintaining, and reviewing information. **Keep your system clean, reliable, and actionable so you can trust the data.**

There are best practice ways to do this, such as data mapping and having a single source of truth. I always recommend periodically doing a simple audit that passes the common-sense test and will go a long way. Invest in resources, outsource, or partner with someone to manage this. This is too important to skip. A blend of internal resources with the latest technology and focused expertise will go a long way.

Stay in control of your data. Otherwise, the tools end up running the process instead of supporting your company's goals. If your CRM data becomes unreliable, you risk losing the ability to track meaningful year-over-year comparisons, and in some cases, you may even need to rebuild your system to regain accuracy.

That's why it's so important to get that right. You want to be able to compare quarters, years, and trends to see if things are going in the right direction. Before automating, first identify the right data and metrics aligned to your strategy. I work with companies to help them focus on these fundamentals as part of a wider GTM strategy. We look at the company goals and then marketing and GTM to support them through the right metrics and data.

Scenario

As part of my business advisory and coaching practice, I help clients not only with their marketing plans but also with setting up for success. One example is having a "growth mindset." I am also part of a think tank networking group of successful businesses and entrepreneurs. We challenge ourselves to look beyond the obvious and what's trending now to help shape what's ahead and how we can help apply it to our businesses and community, such as AI, crypto, talent investment, partnerships, M&A, and more.

The most successful businesses are the ones with a growth mindset. Research psychologist and author Carol Dweck is often credited with coining the term and concept based on extensive work in the field. Carol says, "In a growth mindset, people believe that their most basic abilities can be developed through dedication and hard work—brains and talent are just the starting point."[21] This is in contrast to a "fixed mindset," where the presumption is that we are born with skills and abilities with limited opportunities to change.

Regardless of the different technologies or industries, it really comes down to **perspective, attitude, and vision.** The mechanics and the how are assumed to be there, and it's also assumed that you're going to have a well-oiled machine. But having a healthy mindset about how we want to scale our business is crucial. For example, a lot of businesses go through the transition and recognize, "I can't do everything myself." At this point, they can seek partnerships to bring in specific expertise, hire additional people, invest in technology, or a combination of all. A great analogy I've heard is to think about bringing in "brains" for expertise and "arms and legs" for implementation.

The point is to be clear on what problem you are trying to solve. With the right mindset, clients identify the gaps and needs, such as speed/acceleration

---

[21] Carol S. Dweck, *"Mindset: What Is It?"* (About page, *The Mindset Online*), https://themindsetonline.com/whatisit/about/index.html.

for a new launch, help during a peak time, or rebuilding a process through automation and improved processes for longer-term benefits and improved efficiency.

You may need to put the systems and people in place and make them more interchangeable and repeatable so that the business can be scaled. Take the opportunity to hire people with that growth mindset or partner with companies and consultants who bring you fresh, innovative ideas. Someone with a growth mindset is not transactional. They are not only looking at how things were always done; they want to improve. They want to get better. They want to provide a better experience for the customer.

Think of it as determination and innovation paired with a well-rounded approach, including staying healthy, mentally sharp, and physically energized. Lead with clarity, support your team, and align everyone around a shared vision. When you focus on how you can create value and help others succeed, you naturally position your business for success. That's how I approach my work: by helping other people and companies to grow. At the core, it's all about building strong relationships and continuing to nurture and develop them over time.

I work with clients to help them grow their businesses *without* the stress and overwhelm. Together, we put simple systems in place, use technology to make things easier (not harder), and focus on serving their customers even better, while building a strong foundation for lasting success.

Many times, they are making running changes across the business, from investing in the right systems to leveling up talent, inspiring their clients to do the same. The solutions involved a blend of more strategic thought leadership content and messaging that addressed larger issues, appealing to a senior-level executive audience.

The company delivered strategic business metrics and long-term insights through a business performance dashboard for executive leaders. They stood out from competitors who focused only on current performance and lacked the ability to guide clients in planning two to three years ahead. Automation enabled the executive teams and business owners to step back from daily tasks, allowing them to focus on innovation, spend quality time with customers, and think about the future. Leaders have more time and mental energy to consider: "Where is this business heading?" or "How can my company make a difference?"

The Marketing Formula Brings the Tools and Templates Together

Growth doesn't come without a plan. Clarity drives growth: clarity about the value your business delivers, your direction, and the strategic steps required to move forward with focus and sustain long-term success. Growth also comes from momentum, taking that strategy to market with purpose and precision. Most importantly, growth comes from follow-through, executing in a way that builds value and delivers results you can see and measure.

I created this formula to guide companies through a practical, actionable methodology. At the core, I help tie strategy with execution and leverage systems that support repeatable and lasting success.

There are three core pillars I use.

Three Core Pillars of Strategic Growth

1. Create a Strategic Plan	Start with a solid foundation. A clear strategy sets this foundation, whether your goal is growth, improving customer retention, planning for M&A, or introducing new products/services. Successful leaders start by getting clear on the value they provide, where they are headed, and what it will take to achieve the outcomes. That means aligning business goals with marketing and sales, knowing exactly who you want to reach, and making smart choices about where to focus time and resources for the greatest impact. The best companies and leaders are passionate about their mission and bring heart and soul to the business.
2. Activate the Plan	Once the strategy is in place, it's time to bring it to life in the market. I help companies get traction on their plan by defining go-to-market activations that align marketing, sales, and service teams so the business shows up with purpose, consistency, and credibility. This includes brand positioning, messaging that resonates, offers that connect, and connection efforts that reach the right prospects. Position your business powerfully to engage customers, earn trust, and build

	relationships. Market execution requires a steady presence, showing up with the right message in the right places, to build visibility and momentum that leads to lasting growth.
3. Drive Measurable Outcomes	Strategy and market presence are only as valuable as the results they produce. In my work with companies, I focus on building the practical systems, tools, and structures that turn plans into action and action into measurable success. Specifically, build practical workflows, leverage automation to reduce manual work, and establish performance tracking to evaluate what's working and what isn't. These systems form the basis to incorporate customer feedback and learnings, and adjust based on data and insights. Companies value this approach because it offers more than a strategy; it provides an actionable roadmap that turns plans into results and sustains progress over time.

I apply this three-pillar formula alongside practical experience and strategic partnerships to drive measurable results for companies, whether tech, product- and service-led businesses, or growing small to mid-sized organizations:

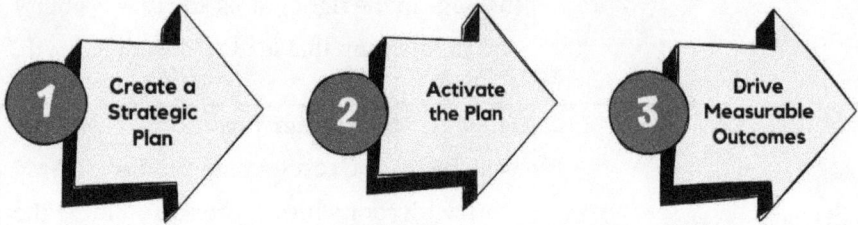

3 Pillar Formula

1	Create a Strategic Plan
2	Activate the Plan
3	Drive Measurable Outcomes

What This Means for You

Having a formula isn't only a process, it's a transformation. The three clear steps bring structure where there's complexity. The formula creates alignment where there are many moving pieces. And it gives leaders the tools to move forward with confidence, knowing their marketing, sales, messaging, and growth plan are all working together. The framework helps you move forward with purpose and alignment.

I am continuously updating my own processes and approach as business needs change, new information is available, I learn more, and new technology enables more capabilities. In my advisory and marketing consulting work, I combine proven, best-in-class tools with my own proprietary methodology, **The Marketing Growth Formula**™ built around driving real business results. The three-pillar formula and approach is a blend of unique templates and frameworks I've developed and updated through my work.

There are two systems in particular that I leverage and cover further in the next chapter: The **Profit Coach**™ **system**[22] from Business Coach Academy, which helps business owners and executives build scalable businesses where they can step out of the daily operations and focus on strategic growth. It's a

---

[22] Business Coach Academy, "The Profit Coach Certified Partner Programme," *Business Coach Academy Blog*, accessed June 5, 2025, https://blog.businesscoachacademy.com/the-profit-coach-certified-partner-programme/.

proven, structured framework to help business owners increase profitability and operational efficiency through personalized strategies, accountability, and expert tools.

Another is the **GTM Operating System** (GTM OS)[23] developed by GTM Partners, created by Sangram Vajre (who authored the Foreword of this book) and Bryan Brown, which helps companies align marketing to broader business objectives with data-driven execution. The GTM OS is a proprietary eight-pillar framework designed to align B2B teams across strategy and execution, enabling scalable, efficient revenue growth.

For my own proprietary frameworks, I adapt strategies for real-world application, including investing in new markets, brand positioning, messaging and GTM planning to get results and grow profitably.

It's incredibly rewarding to work alongside clients to accelerate their results. I bring together proven tools, practical templates, and customized strategies shaped by my experience as a CMO. We focus on what will move their business forward, avoid common pitfalls, and build marketing strategies that drive lasting, profitable growth. The combination of technology, process, and people is powerful.

Technology tip: Map out your "tech stack."
Tip

When it comes to technology, one tip that I'll leave you with is to map out your tech stack, your tools, and technology platforms. The companies I work with are usually surprised to see the long list. Make a list and review:

- Name of the tool, supplier.
- If a subscription, what is the length? (Note any discounts for buying for one, two, or three-year commitments.)

---

[23] GTM Partners, *Home*, accessed June 5, 2025, https://gtmpartners.com/.

- What's your monthly spend on each?
- What are the business benefits of each of those programs?
- What's missing? What's not on your list? Categorize by *need,* not application.
- Which areas need further review or expertise to review the list?
- Outcomes: Start by looking at how your team is leveraging the technology, including AI.
- How effective are these tools (versus adding time/cost)? Do they save you costs in other areas? Do they help you reach your goals?

A simple inventory is all it takes to get started. Based on my experience, I help clients assess what's effective, where to invest, and where it could make sense to scale back.

The process begins with understanding your business goals. Next, we can map the ROI of the systems, which many business professionals can overlook. Don't leave all the technology responsibilities to the IT team or the CIO. While the IT team can set up and maintain the systems, it is the responsibility of marketing, sales, go-to-market (GTM) experts, and business owners to drive the desired outcomes and results and to determine whether the technology meets their needs.

Tech Path Ahead for Marketing

Let's talk about where technology is going, specifically for marketers. I hear this question/comment a lot. Though none of us has the magic answer, certain elements will be *timeless,* such as solving problems for your market, staying on top of shifting needs, and building true relationships.

It's already happening today, but within the next two to three years, more of these **platforms will come together into a better workflow** (literally flow of work). We just talked about this with tech stacks. We won't need to assemble our own complex tech stacks; we will be able to focus more on our business outcomes, and the technology will be further integrated. It's already happening.

I do think buyers will always be somewhat cautious about going all-in, though, with one supplier. There's a trade-off between having the kind of individual products that you stitch together versus the other extreme of investing with one company for their platform. The classic question of "best of breed" versus platform.

What I see happening, though, is that tech is becoming more modular and interchangeable. It is kind of crazy that we have to tie so much together today. We'll look back and say, "I remember when companies had to buy all these individual subscriptions and band them together."

I think our technical calories in the future will be spent more on what the solutions are *doing* for us. We won't have to figure out automation as much, tie things together, or make sure there are the right interfaces or APIs between programs. That will definitely become more of a given in the future. Then, we're going to spend more of our efforts on leveraging large language models, customizing them for our business, or using our own autonomous AI agents.

AI is a massive part of this shift, and cannot be underestimated. But still, at the heart is human problem-solving to know what challenges exist before applying the technology. AI agents are increasingly becoming part of how businesses operate, such as supporting decision-making and execution. But I'm even more bullish on the *human side* in business. As AI continues to evolve and integrate even further into everyday business, the real differentiator will be how effectively professionals apply the technology. We need to **develop the skill** to map AI with human insight, leadership, and creativity. The strongest companies will be those that combine the best of human traits with the efficiency of AI. And, the technology plays together so that we won't have to spend so much strategic time and budget pulling it all together.

Looking past the tools, we can integrate core technologies and see how AI can work for us. AI is clearly helping tackle some of the bigger challenges in our world, such as improving therapeutics development, strengthening cybersecurity, and making blockchain more usable in real-world ways. We won't have to *know* all the technical details, but we will need to lead and drive how these models are shaped and used.

Freeing Up Humans

By leveraging technology and doing our part, we'll be able to spend more time on some of those problem sets and other factors within the world's problems. I am inspired by the possibilities ahead, not only by where AI is going but also by the fact that we all have a role in shaping it. This isn't something happening *to us*; it's something we have the opportunity to help build.

Another way to think of this is in a generational context. Technology is moving at lightning speed. What we were born with and learned becomes a given for the next generation. One of the extraordinary aspects is that we can witness these massive shifts firsthand. That's why I went through the different industrial phases.

The other piece on the human side is the workforce. Everyone comes with their own perspective. People of all ages are using tech. It's not always generational, but the exposure to it is what I want to draw out. Exposure and experience differ by generation. That's one of the really great things about keeping yourself abreast of technology, the latest trends, and what's happening to a certain degree, because then you can relate as some of those shifts are happening.

At the same time, thanks to technology's accessibility, there has never been a better opportunity to build connections and partnerships. The model of working for one company for many years has shifted, making it easier than ever to start or grow a business.

Even within companies, professionals can apply entrepreneurial thinking and innovation. You don't have to choose whether to work for a company or for yourself; both paths offer opportunities to innovate, commercialize ideas, and drive change. What matters most is the range of experiences and perspectives each individual brings. The rapid changes in technology, processes, and the expertise applied make **this an exciting time to be in business, an exciting time to be alive.**

CHAPTER 8

WHERE WILL YOU TAKE YOUR BUSINESS NEXT?

Together, we've explored the core elements of marketing, including defining your ideal customer profile, positioning your brand, crafting compelling messaging, and building a strong go-to-market plan. All of this is grounded in data and supported by analytics to inform decisions and track performance. Next, we'll focus on where you want to take your business from here by applying the ideas and concepts we've covered. Thinking ahead a few steps will dramatically help you with the strategy, actions, investments, and shifts that you need to make.

Where do you want that to be? The answer will inform your marketing and business strategy today. Whatever we're doing now, we know that's going to be different a year from now, five years from now, ten years from now, and even more so with the pace of change, the pace of technology.

Your customers are going to be more advanced. Teams will be further developed, but there will be market changes, new problems to solve, and new opportunities for you and your business. And, there's always an opportunity to review and increase market presence.

The business ownership or executive level could change. You may be looking at an exit, merger or acquisition, expansion, or other changes. You might even be looking for location or lifestyle changes.

But there will be changes, and the world around us is changing rapidly. Ironically, many of the fundamentals will stay the same.

Core Foundations

Of course, technology will continue at a rapid pace, especially AI. Yet, some of the foundational pieces won't change. Let's look at a few of those: First, I believe the human connection will stay strong at some level. The essence of this is the need to listen to your customers and hear their needs, solve their problems, and win their hearts and minds, especially in a data-driven world. Companies spend a lot on brands, but truly and authentically connecting with customers is what drives the brand and experience. There is constant discussion about the possibility of AI replacing humans. But I remain bullish on the human side, a collaboration between humans and AI. Humans have the heart and soul that technology can't replicate.

Company and personal values will need to endure, because they can evolve while staying true to their core. Sometimes, companies dilute these messages to the point where they all sound the same. They treat the messages as a checkbox exercise to pump out content and lose the real meaning behind them. Instead, let your customers experience your brand and value through authenticity, quality, and integrity.

You also want your employees to experience these values firsthand. Today, there's a greater appreciation than ever for companies that genuinely live their values and share a greater purpose. I expect that to continue.

The same is true for having **goals and dreams.** Of course, these will change over time, but the underlying motivation remains the same. For example, we aspire to make a difference, help businesses grow, solve challenges for our customers, invest in our communities, and uplift our teams. That commitment to having a real impact is unwavering.

A successful business will always have new goals, ways to deliver on a vision, and ways to build on dreams. Maybe that vision is about making the world better in some way, driving profitability, creating new opportunities, or helping customers solve critical challenges. But the real win comes when you help your customers solve *their* problems. That creates a lasting impact, a ripple effect that moves outward like a pebble dropped in a pond. It's an exciting and motivating way to think about our work.

Another constant is **time**. We all have the same twenty-four hours in a day. When you stop and think about it, how you invest your time and who you invest it with is one of the most powerful choices you can make. Time truly is the great equalizer.

How are you using your time? There's really no right answer, but think about it for a minute. Some business owners want more free time, others want to generate more revenue, or expand their market. For a leader who wants more time, they may need more automation to create that extra time for their family or to start another business. Maybe they just want to catch their breath, pursue a hobby, or care for a child or ill parent. Others might want to use that time to build, create, pray, meditate, travel, or exercise.

Again, it could be starting that next business. It could be learning from a mentor or pursuing a dream. But what does that look like? If you think about it, isn't that why businesses focus on efficiency with time? Because time itself cannot be increased.

That's why so many companies make claims such as "40% savings with automation" or demonstrate how to help you gain more time back through AI. It's beyond pure dollar savings, although that's important to any business. It's also about saving time. Think about the opportunity cost. Where else could you spend your time, and how will that impact your business? Time is a precious resource.

There will also continue to be a strong need for a clear value proposition. What value do you provide, and how are you different from others in the market? AI and tech can help you compare and analyze, but your true value proposition still comes from leadership, from the business owner or CEO, based on an understanding of the market. The need for clear distinction and positioning of the brand or portfolio will remain critical in the near term.

There will also always be a need to reach new customers and build new business transactions. The way we do that might change; technology, AI, and new work processes are already reshaping roles and methods. But if you step back, the goal remains the same: reaching new customers and communicating what your brand, product, or service is all about. While the formats and tools may evolve, the core stays constant: connecting buyers and sellers.

What's Changing?

Now, let's look at what's changing. Very specifically, automation and AI are being implemented to completely disrupt the way we operate, starting with manual tasks and workflow. There shouldn't have to be re-entry of data or manually porting information between systems. We need to provide information in one place, one format, and then enable the technology to move, update, repurpose, combine, and work with that data. For example, if you are creating a thought leadership article, the systems should be able to parse that into other formats, such as emails targeted to different roles, or social media posts, or become the script for a video. Then, you can turn that video into webinar or podcast content, and move straight into reels or shorts for posts.

But how do you categorize customer interest? Marketing shouldn't need to spend as much time reconnecting the same pipes. We're moving toward more content and compelling messaging. Two-way and multi-way conversations with customers, partners, and the market will only increase. We saw it with social media, but AI is going to allow even more conversations with customers. We're seeing it with AI bots being able to handle those first few levels, even setting up meetings. Again, with this plumbing concept, our systems can answer some of the most basic questions to make humans more available for strategic work and talking with real customers.

I'm optimistic about the hyper-personalization of marketing. What does that really mean? Think about how you feel when you receive a message or hear from a company. Of course, you'll give it more attention if it's relevant. Does the message resonate with you? Does the message show that the company understands you and the challenges you or your company face? I think there's been an overemphasis in the past on the demographics, firmographics, and a company's location to demonstrate that a seller knows something about them. Prospects will identify much more deeply with messages that speak to understanding and solving their **problem set** over reflecting back basic firmographic info.

For example, you may know that their accounting team is overloaded with invoices. It's important to show that you understand the realities your audience faces. Technical teams and CIOs are overwhelmed with technology and are working hard to modernize systems and support the accounting teams in this example. Leaders seek ways to claw back time, operate more efficiently, and focus on growing their businesses. Many are frustrated by the reality of having advanced tools while still needing to port over information manually, wasting time, money, and opportunity costs. To break through, we need to reach the right decision-maker, whether it's a business leader in accounting or a leader in IT. When we show that we understand the challenge, can offer real solutions, and have delivered measurable results for others, we position ourselves as the best partner for the job.

True personalization connects you with that right person facing the problem, where you can offer a relevant solution. That's why personalization, and especially hyper-personalization, matters so much in marketing today. At the same time, stay aware of data privacy regulations and best practices. Tailored messaging should feel helpful and not invasive.

Once you can narrow in on understanding the problem set and demonstrate that you can add value, you'll have more credibility, and your ideal customer will want to engage. Overall, you can create a better buying experience and set up for a longer-term relationship.

Customer expectations are only going to increase. B2B buyers are also consumers in their personal lives. They see an e-commerce site that's easy, a one-click, and we expect that to happen in the business world and government world as well. And why shouldn't they expect this experience?

Technology Shifts Continue

Of course, technology will continue to drive change and disruption. AI isn't a trend; it's a foundational shift that is completely reshaping how we live and work. Generative AI is already delivering real results at lightning speed, and AI agents are quickly moving beyond isolated tasks into coordinated, orchestrated workflows. This means the agents are becoming more autonomous and can operate as digital workers.

The next phase isn't just about what AI can do in isolation; it will focus on how these systems connect, interact, and make decisions across tools and teams. And still, we're in the early phase of AI widespread adoption, with far more to come. But for AI to drive real results, it needs to be integrated and applied thoughtfully. Some companies are still running pilots and trying to identify the best use cases, but I encourage you to think bigger: focus on what technology can actually do for you and your teams and for your customers to bring about the best experience possible.

Where do you want to position yourself in this shift? Will you be someone who uses AI? Someone who benefits from it, or maybe creates with AI? We need to be leveling up our knowledge and continuing to learn, or we will fall behind. But that doesn't mean you have to become an AI expert. It might simply mean knowing enough to partner with the right experts who can help you bridge the gaps. You don't have the time to master everything; none of us do. That's why it's critical to be clear about where you want to be the expert, where you add the most value, and where you should partner. Consider where it makes sense to bring in outside expertise, saving both time and money in the long run.

In my experience, leveraging AI in marketing is already making a real difference, helping teams work smarter, move faster, and increase productivity where it counts.

IDC, a very trusted market analyst in technology and business, estimates that generative AI will increase marketing productivity by more than 40% by 2029.[24] Although this will eliminate some activities and roles, it will also open up new opportunities and roles.

While this is specific to marketing and cumulative over several years, this is significant because, since the 1950s, productivity has typically ranged between 1.5% and 2.9%, as reported by the Economic Strategy Group.[25] But the point is that we're seeing unprecedented productivity increases and savings in companies. That's why AI is so transformative. The difference is our ability and capacity to operationalize strategy with greater precision and impact. Momentum leads to transformation, and real-time, adaptive execution sets companies apart.

---

[24] IDC, "IDC Forecasts Global ICT Spending to Reach $5.1 Trillion in 2024," *International Data Corporation (IDC)*, accessed March 2025, https://www.idc.com/getdoc.jsp?containerId=prUS51999824.

[25] Aspen Economic Strategy Group, "In Brief: U.S. Labor Productivity," *Aspen Economic Strategy Group*, accessed March 2025, https://www.economicstrategygroup.org/publication/in-brief-us-labor-productivity/.

I believe partnerships, technology, and improved workflows aren't simply nice to have. These essential elements give you back time, energy, and help create a thriving, profitable business.

A Roadmap to Success

No matter what industry you serve or the size of your company, the basic business mechanics are often the same. Sales and marketing are a major part of any business, and a giant lever for revenue, customer fulfillment, new business, brand, and GTM. Building and maintaining or growing a successful business starts with all teams focused on common company goals and metrics. Excellence in functions today (whether marketing, sales, finance, HR, engineering, operations, etc.) contributes to the success, but the interaction between the roles changes as customer needs change. For example, marketing, sales, and customer success are tied together even more closely for revenue operations and GTM strategies, roles, and capabilities that continue to evolve. The teams came together under a common shared goal for measurable pipeline and revenue. Today's most successful leaders have a growth mindset, lead high-performing teams, drive results, and collaborate across the business to create real momentum. When teams are aligned, accountable, and have a strategic voice at the table, they don't just keep up, they thrive. The goal is to serve the market with clarity, purpose, and continuing value. That's where real growth happens.

As work becomes more connected, distributed, and intelligent, leadership in B2B companies must evolve alongside it. Innovation now draws from an even broader spectrum; ideas can come from a much wider field. AI and intelligent systems help us scale faster, connect deeper, and drive change across the business. Outcomes are shaped by how well leaders integrate technology, harness AI, and tap into flexible talent models like fractional teams and strategic partners. The *way* we work has fundamentally shifted. Outcomes now depend on a blend of employees, fractional experts, automation, and AI agents working in sync. The team depends on how well human and intelligent systems collaborate to deliver results. The technology powering business combines internal platforms, on-premise systems, cloud solutions, subscription tools, specialized services, and more. Success and results come from effectively integrating these technologies to empower human and AI workers to execute, adapt, and scale together.

Leading in this environment means helping people work smarter, removing friction, and making sure everyone stays aligned on what matters most. The leaders who thrive focus on guiding teams toward meaningful outcomes. They'll use real-time insights, shared context, and the right tools to support faster, better decisions that are truly centered on the market and customers. The best leaders will still motivate people, but they will also design environments where people and intelligent systems work in sync to deliver value faster and smarter.

This shift won't eliminate the need for vision or strategic thinking; it will elevate strategy. In B2B, where buying decisions are complex and cycles are long, the companies that win will be those led by teams that can act quickly, stay aligned on value, and adapt their approach without losing focus.

Frameworks and Tools on the Roadmap

Scaling a business profitably takes more than ambition; it requires a clear, strategic path forward. I use several proven frameworks in my advisory and coaching work that help companies take strategic steps toward profitable growth. One example is the **nine-step roadmap**, developed by the Business Coach Academy under the Profit Coach™ system, which helps business owners and leaders scale effectively by setting up their businesses for long-term success. Whether a small business or a growing enterprise, leaders can relate to the need to operationalize their business and not be at the center of every move. Together, we look at sales and marketing systems in place and how to automate and scale with the human elements that are timeless.

The Profit Coach 9-Step Roadmap

(Graphic provided by Business Coach Academy)

The GTM (Go-to-Market) Operating System

The GTM Operating System™ from GTM Partners is a unified framework designed to help companies drive revenue with clarity, consistency, and cross-functional alignment. Built around eight critical areas: Total Relevant Market, Market Investment, Brand and Demand, Pipeline, Customer Time-to-Value, Customer Expansion, Revenue Operations, and Leadership & Management, the system provides a common approach and language to ensure every team operates from the same strategic foundation. The GTM Operating System helps teams ask the right questions and evaluate the most critical aspects, such as: Where can you grow the most? What is the ROI in the customer's mind? Which GTM metrics drive your business health? And which product or service creates the highest customer value? By addressing these core components, companies can align their go-to-market efforts, improve efficiency, and accelerate growth. Our computers and phones have operating systems; why shouldn't our businesses?

As a certified GTM Partner, I help companies implement this framework in a way that's tailored to their market and growth stage, connecting strategy with execution to unlock real, measurable results.

(Graphic provided by GTM Partners)

Chart Your Course and Define What's Next

It doesn't matter whether you're working for a company, running your own business, or thinking about starting one. There's never been a better time to pursue an entrepreneurial path, build meaningful relationships with companies, and drive new revenue streams.

Think about what you want to create and the purpose. Maybe you want to have more free time to raise a family, spend time with aging parents, express your creativity, build on a hobby, travel, or give to your church or community. Or maybe you would like to have more time to build another business, or level up your business to be more profitable and increase revenue. Define what you want to build or create. What is that goal? Define your pillars, purpose, and financial needs, and think about time, family, location, and what inspires you the most.

There has been a major shift in how and where we work, from relocating to hybrid models and remote work. Today, you can hire talent and serve clients around the world. There has never been a time with this level of opportunity, tools, and support. Technology plays a massive role, but the communities, focused industry groups, and networks that help you build and scale are equally important.

Scenario

Through my consulting and business advisory, I've seen and helped several new businesses get off the ground, establishing a vision, marketing strategy, pitch deck, research plan, and creating offers. What do most of these businesses have in common?

A core theme that emerged was the desire for personal freedom. Each business owner dreamed about creating their own opportunities in some way. Each person recognized that the journey would have challenges; none of them were under any illusions and firmly believed a new business was the right path. The broader environment has changed as well, with more frequent job shifts, increased offshoring, and a rise in corporate structures. Still, there are more opportunities than ever and more ways to apply talent in meaningful ways.

Some of my clients felt that running their own businesses actually gave them more freedom and stability. Many appreciated the corporate roles, especially the experience that gave them the brands, the access, and the cutting-edge skills. But now they were ready and wanted to strike out on their own. However, sometimes they didn't know how to get started. Several of them wanted marketing and GTM consulting for a foundation. Many of them needed a marketing strategy and a plan.

I have found it incredibly rewarding to help businesses launch and grow profitably. I was honored to receive U.S. Coach of the Year from the Business Coach Academy. While that recognition means a lot to me, the true reward has always been helping my clients succeed. Whether through marketing consulting, business advisory, or coaching, I love watching my clients build momentum and create a real impact for their teams and their customers.

I wanted to share these insights from others because they underscore something even more significant: the remarkable number of new businesses being formed today and the unprecedented access entrepreneurs have to resources, tools, and support. I am grateful to help and be part of their journey.

Anticipating Market Needs

Anticipating marketing needs is very important, too. If you think about where your business is going next, you need to continue to consider the market needs, as we talked about in Chapter 1. Your customers' needs are changing, too, of course. They're always looking at new ways to innovate and solve new problems and challenges. As you help them solve one problem, there's the next problem and the next hurdle. But that's all part of progress, and that's all part of development.

Stay close to your customers and prospects, and notice how their pain points are evolving. The real goal is to be proactive: anticipate future challenges based on your experience and expertise, and position yourself to meet those needs before they arise.

I work with clients every day to help them build a strategic foundation, starting with a clear marketing plan, a deep understanding of their customers, and a realistic view of market opportunities. It's not enough to have a website or a CRM system. Businesses need a thoughtful approach to connect with their market, position their brand effectively, and translate that strategy into coordinated actions across channels. Do they know who their prime market is, the target buyer within that market? Where can they expand next? Are their marketing channels aligned to support the customer journey and business goals?

Think about building for the future and stability, especially if you're creating your own business. Starting a business is definitely not for everyone. There are many areas to address, such as taxes, insurance, marketing, sales, hiring, operations, etc. Starting a business is also an exciting opportunity and way forward. If starting a business or refreshing a business is in your heart and something that you want to do, I can help you with that.

Think about what you're creating for the market and ask yourself, *What does my business actually do? Where can we provide the most value?* Be reflective and think about why you created your business, whether you're a CEO, new business owner, or working within a company. Always think about it.

If you're a professional working within a company, you can still think like an entrepreneur. In many ways, your primary client is the organization itself. Many people think that entrepreneurs are people who create their own businesses, but there are absolutely ways you can be entrepreneurial within a company and innovate. Are you working to create new opportunities within your company, such as expanding into adjacent markets, leading new initiatives, solving challenges, or building stronger teams? You may want to level up your skills to advance, make a difference for customers, or a combination. Determine what drives you to help you shape your future path and focus on what will matter most over time.

Tying It All Together

Let's look back at what we covered and tie it all together. Successful businesses depend on a consistent, effective revenue stream and delighted customers. Winning go-to-market motions rely on solid, effective marketing working with sales to drive customer acquisition, accelerate revenue growth, and enhance customer retention.

"When marketing aligns closely with GTM objectives, it becomes a strategic engine that attracts the right customers, delivers clear value, and fosters lasting relationships. Precise, measurable strategies such as focused positioning to show clearly what your company provides, compelling messaging that resonates, integrated channel execution, and ongoing performance analysis, set impactful marketing apart from ineffective efforts."

I created the following graphic to articulate and highlight the difference based on my experience.

Effective, Intentional
- Starts with a marketing strategy
- Human led, connect with market
- Automate where possible
- GTM plan, connect messages across channels
- Analytics to measure results, adjust course

Ineffective, Reactive
- Random acts of marketing, lacks strategy
- Highly reactive, chasing 'squirrels'
- Volume-based outreach
- Cranking out content, see what sticks
- Lack of measures, metrics

Here's a summary look back at the key ideas we've covered. Each chapter offers a distinct layer that can support your next stage or provide a new perspective on marketing and GTM. Together, these concepts interweave change and innovation with timeless, foundational principles: the balance that fuels enduring growth.

Market intelligence: We started in Chapter 1 with market intelligence. Know your market, the needs, problem sets, and alternative solutions. To truly understand your customers, track and apply the impacts of economic policy and industry changes. Stay informed about the environment your customers experience and help them align their business to these changes. As hockey legend Wayne Gretzky famously said, "Skate to where the puck is going to be, not where it has been."[26]

Positioning: In Chapter 2, we covered positioning your brand, product, or service. Where can you add the most value? How are you different from other alternatives in the market? Before you get to positioning, you would have already firmed up the size of your market and considered how widespread this problem is and what the customer base is willing to pay. Marketing sizing and positioning are very important steps before diving into messaging.

Messaging: Now that you are clear on the market size and how you offer different value than others, we looked at how you can communicate your brand, product, or service to these ideal customers in a way that resonates with them. We also explored different formats based on the market and provided these customers with informative, consistent messages and content.

Go-to-Market (GTM) activations or motions: Now that you have an understanding of the market and how you're positioned, messaging and communicating with your market, it's time to look at the specific GTM activations in channels. This is a blend of marketing and sales. We covered

---

[26] Wayne Gretzky, "I skate to where the puck is going to be, not where it has been," *BrainyQuote*, accessed June 5, 2025, https://www.brainyquote.com/quotes/wayne_gretzky_383282.

several approaches, such as outbound or reaching out, inbound, which is what's coming into your company based on what you put out there, account-based marketing (ABM), events, partnerships, community-based go-to-market, and product- or service-led go-to-market motions. The GTM motion is the approach to reaching your customers. GTM is actually a much broader category encompassing strategy and growth. In this context, we are exploring GTM channels.

People: Chapter 5 highlighted the distinct capabilities of human talent, from adaptable thinking and emotional intelligence to relationship-building that drives trust and collaboration. We build strong connections, develop talent, and leverage partnerships and technology to enhance performance. In a fast-paced, automated world, we focus on authenticity to win hearts and minds.

Measuring Results: Chapter 6 covered measuring results and outcomes, using analytics to deliver insights, and assessing performance. What's working? Where do you need to make adjustments? The performance measures and metrics inform your strategy and help you adjust your course. Select the right metrics that are tied to company performance but specific enough to measure momentum.

Technology and Process: Finally, we looked at technology and process or workflow. Together, they play a foundational role. What's the role of technology in helping your business? Having a certain level of tech understanding is important in the same way that being financially savvy is critical to the business. We talked about how tech is everywhere today; we are on the brink of a new era with data and AI. The process or workflow is fundamental to success here because either the technology needs to fit around the process today, the process needs to adapt to the best practices used with the technology, or both. Map your processes and workflow before implementing new technology or automation to better streamline and have the technology work for you and your team. Create a form of governance or procedures to maintain the data.

Automation, AI, and the marketing tech stack applications and platforms are all areas that can help your business when used and leveraged in the right way. The key is to leverage AI, technology, and automation effectively and to partner with an expert who supports your business without overwhelming you. There are capabilities in each of these sub-areas of technology, and the marketing technology stack.

In this chapter, we explored how to define what's next for your business and create a forward-looking plan to put these concepts into practice and turn ideas into action. Despite the rapid changes and continual upheaval, several fundamental elements will remain central. At the core are **human connection, authenticity, and innovation.**

You have an opportunity to define what your business and future will look like, whether it's growth, profit, a business exit, a balanced life, mentorship, paying it forward, or a blend of several. There's a lot here, but this is an area where we can work together.

It's been a powerful journey, and it's only beginning.

CONCLUSION

Marketing drives the business forward, guiding strategy, fueling demand, and influencing how buyers make decisions. What really matters now is how you choose to **show up** in your market and what value your company brings. With a clearer view of how marketing can deliver and how it connects to the business measures, **you can prioritize what works for your market**, build authentic relationships, and lead with purpose. Mindset is half the battle to set up for success.

Look at where you can make a difference. Think about a strategic plan; there's always time for strategy. When you make time for strategy upfront, you set the stage for smoother execution, fewer setbacks, and lasting results. Create a thoughtful plan for successful implementation and delivery.

Now, you should have a greater appreciation for the depth of marketing, GTM, and connection to the business strategy. You recognize the importance of consistency, a multi-channel approach, and authentic communication to build lasting customer relationships over time. This approach will always outperform the "shiny objects" that often distract, like "chasing a jumping squirrel."

Now that you've gained an appreciation and understanding of strategy and tactics, measuring, and adjusting course, my hope is that you can apply this knowledge to contribute to your efforts in building a business and life that you love.

I'm really excited about what's possible as you build this foundation. I'm optimistic about what lies ahead and the potential for us to take this further together. You now have a solid baseline understanding, and I'd love to work with you to apply these concepts.

Thank you for going on this journey together. It's been an honor to provide insights and share my own perspectives and experience. This is really the start of a bigger journey. Since you picked up this book, it means you're interested in further developing yourself and your business, helping your clients, or it could be "digging out from under." Maybe you're overwhelmed and want a more balanced lifestyle. Perhaps you wanted to understand more about the mystique of marketing and GTM. Regardless of the reason, you took an important step. This book adds one piece to the puzzle to help you become more informed and connected.

Let's get your strategic marketing plan in place so you can have the business you deserve, serve the clients at the level you want to, build that stellar reputation, be profitable, and live your dreams with a fulfilling business purpose.

That's what this is about. You're creating opportunities for yourself, your family, your team members, and your clients. It really has that ripple effect we talked about, with the pebble in the pond and the concentric circle. That's what's exciting to me.

Applying the understanding, the latest tools, and operating with these new approaches requires continued refinement and learning. Business development, providing great marketing, and go-to-market are in my blood. I love and thrive on helping companies craft those practical strategies and plans to help make them heard, and ultimately more profitable.

Leverage authentic marketing strategies while you incorporate new concepts; that's how you'll stay constant and relevant at the forefront of the market.

I set up my business to create and build momentum. I truly believe in the saying that a rising tide lifts all boats, and I'm doing my part to help lift boats. You are, too. When one business grows, it lifts others around it. I want to help you apply these concepts so you can get a return on the marketing investments you're making, consider the right strategies, and achieve the lifestyle and level of profitability you desire.

Wherever you are in your journey, you can put these ideas into action in a way that works for you, making marketing investments that deliver returns at every level.

I've seen how the right marketing strategy can spark growth, improve profitability, and open new possibilities, whether you're growing a business, starting something new, or preparing for an exit.

Let's move forward strategically, confidently, and with purpose.

Tip: Stay informed and never stop learning.

Tip

I have one final tip and idea. I want you to identify three important initiatives that will help your business.

For example, is an updated marketing strategy what's most critical to you? Do you need to refine your ideal customer profile or brand positioning in the market? Maybe you need analytics or a GTM dashboard. Or it could be a referral program or high-value thought leadership content that resonates with executive audiences. What's going to really make a difference for you? Of course, you need a strategy, but beyond that, do you need to look at hiring or partnerships?

Give that a little bit of thought and consider what problem or challenge you are trying to solve, just as you would solve problems and challenges for your customers. Then, take action and write down those three initiatives with an approximate timeline. This simple step will help you move from thoughts to action.

It's a pleasure to be on this journey with you. I'm so excited about your business and *your* future, and what the marketing growth formula can do for you.

There's a real opportunity in front of you, and you're ready to turn it into a lasting impact with the right formula.

I wish you all the best in your business and your life. This is not the end...

This is just the beginning.

THANK YOU FOR READING MY BOOK!

DOWNLOAD YOUR FREE GIFTS

As a thank-you for purchasing and reading my book, I'd love to share some additional tools and resources you can start using today to help plan your business. You'll also find details to schedule a welcome call.

Scan the QR Code:

themarketinggrowthformula.com

I would appreciate it if you could leave your invaluable review on Amazon.com.
Thank you!

www.ingramcontent.com/pod-product-compliance
Lightning Source LLC
Chambersburg PA
CBHW031504180326
41458CB00044B/6688/J